AIR FRYER

RECIPES

COOKBOOK

The ultimate Guide to Flavorful Air Fryer
Recipes for Healthier you

JAMES K. THOMAS

TABLE OF CONTENTS

INTRODUCTION

The ability of an air fryer to cook food more healthily and practically has led to its meteoric rise in popularity in recent years. It is a countertop appliance that uses hot air circulation to cook a variety of foods, producing a meal that is crispy and tasty and resembles deep-fried food but uses much less oil.

The sophisticated cooking technique of an air fryer is its fundamental idea. A strong heating element and a fast fan are both included in the device, and they combine to quickly circulate the air. When the air fryer is switched on, the heating element quickly warms the air within the frying chamber, and the fan uniformly disperses this heated air around the food that is put in the fryer's basket or tray.

One of the main advantages of utilizing an air fryer is that it uses a lot less oil than conventional frying techniques to prepare meals. In actuality, the term "air fryer" refers to a cooking device that utilizes hot air instead of a lot of oil to fry food. The air fryer creates a crispy coating while retaining the natural juices and flavors of the contents by depending on hot air circulation.

Air fryers provide several additional benefits in addition to using less oil. Compared to a normal oven, they provide a speedier cooking experience since the hot air moves about the food more effectively. For busy people or families that want simple, fast meals, this might be extremely useful. Additionally, air fryers are adaptable kitchen machines that can cook a range of foods, such as doughnuts, apple fritters, chicken wings, vegetables, seafood, and even sweets like French fries and chicken wings.

Additionally well renowned for their user-friendly characteristics are air fryers. They often include temperature-adjustable settings, enabling you to change the cooking temperature following the demands of the recipe. Many versions come with an integrated timer that turns the fryer off automatically when the cooking time is up, eliminating overcooking or burning. Some high-tech air fryers also have pre-programmed cooking settings for certain foods, making it even simpler to get reliable and delectable results.

An air fryer is often easy to clean as well. It is often possible to detach the cooking basket or tray, which contains the food, and wash it separately, either by hand or in the dishwasher. The outside of the fryer may be cleaned with a wet cloth, making maintenance simple and extending the life of the equipment.

Although air fryers have gained enormous popularity because of their convenience and health-conscious ethos, it's crucial to remember that they may not be appropriate for all culinary tasks. Typically battered or highly coated foods cannot have the same texture and crispiness as deep-fried foods. However, a variety of meals may provide pleasing outcomes with a little experimenting and adjusting.

ADVANTAGES OF COOKING WITH AN AIR FRYER

✓ **Healthier Cooking:** One of the main advantages of using an air fryer is that you may enjoy delicious, crispy dishes while using a lot less oil. A comparable texture and flavor to typical deep-fried dishes are produced by air fryers using hot air circulation and a little quantity of oil but with up to 80% less fat. Those who are seeking to cut down on their consumption of fat or calories may find this to be helpful.

✓ **Reduced Risk of Health Problems:** Cooking using an air fryer may help lower the risk of several health problems linked to excessive oil intake by using less oil. It may support enhancing overall cardiovascular health, lowering the risk of heart disease, and maintaining healthy cholesterol levels.

Air fryers are very adaptable kitchen gadgets that can perform a range of culinary activities. They can grill, bake, roast, cook, and even reheat meals. Air fryers provide a variety of cooking possibilities to accommodate various tastes and preferences, from crunchy French fries and chicken wings to roasted veggies and baked delicacies.

✓ *Efficiency in terms of time:* Air fryers are renowned for their quick cooking periods. They are a time-saving alternative for those who are busy since they warm rapidly and cook meals more quickly than conventional ovens. Additionally, because of their small size, quicker heat transfer is possible, resulting in more evenly and effectively cooked food.

✓ *Energy Efficiency:* Since air fryers need less energy to heat up and cook food, they are more energy-efficient than conventional ovens. They also use less power due to their compact size. This may help you save money on electricity and lessen your environmental impact.

✓ **_Simple to Use and Clean:_** Air fryers are designed to be simple to use and need little effort to maintain. The majority of models include simple controls and pre-programmed settings, making it simple to choose the preferred cooking time and temperature. Additionally, air fryers often have non-stick frying surfaces that can be readily cleaned with a damp cloth or put in the dishwasher.

✓ **_Safety precautions:_** Air fryers include several built-in safety precautions, including temperature controls and timers with automatic shut-offs. These characteristics lessen the possibility of mishaps in the kitchen by preventing food from being overcooked or burned.

✓ **_Reduction of odors:_** Traditional deep-frying might leave your kitchen smelling bad for a while. Cooking using air fryers results in substantially fewer unpleasant cooking smells.

✓ *Space-saving:* Compared to conventional ovens or deep fryers, air fryers are small kitchen equipment that needs less room. Smaller homes or those with limited kitchen space can particularly benefit from this.

✓ *Family-friendly:* Air fryers are excellent for families since you can make healthier variations of common fried items that both kids and adults will like. It's a great way to get your family started on healthy eating habits without compromising on flavor.

ADVICE FOR COOKING WITH AN AIR FRYER

✓ Pre-heating your air fryer is crucial, just as with conventional cooking techniques. This shortens the total cooking time while ensuring that your food cooks evenly.

✓ Utilize the proper temperature: Traditional ovens normally cook at a lower temperature than air fryers. For the greatest results, it's crucial to adhere to the suggested temperature settings for various recipes. To avoid overcooking or burning, it's always a good idea to keep an eye on your food.

✓ Avoid packing the air fryer basket too tightly for proper air circulation and consistent frying. Allow enough room around your meal so that hot air can travel around each item, resulting in crispy and uniformly cooked results.

✓ Shake or rotate your meal halfway through cooking to make sure it cooks evenly. This makes it easier to have a crispy, golden exterior on both sides.

✓ Use a little oil spray: Even though air frying is renowned for its capacity to cook food with little oil, applying a light oil spray may improve the flavor and crispiness of certain items. Popular options include coconut oil, avocado oil, and olive oil. To keep your meal from being greasy, just make sure to use a modest quantity.

✓ Try different spices and marinades: Air frying is flexible and offers many flavor options. To improve the flavor of your food, don't be hesitant to experiment with various flavors, spices, and marinades. Due to the possibility of extremely fine granules blowing about in the air fryer, pay attention to the texture of the spice you use.

✓ Maintaining the efficiency of your air fryer and avoiding any unpleasant odors requires regular cleaning. Make care to clean and dry any detachable components according to the manufacturer's cleaning recommendations.

✓ Adapt cooking times and temperatures: The cooking times and temperatures for various air fryer models may vary somewhat. It's crucial to pay attention to the directions for your particular model and make modifications as necessary. To ensure that your food is cooked to the proper degree of doneness, keep a constant check on it and, if necessary, use a kitchen thermometer.

✓ Make up your recipes; air fryers aren't simply for frying conventional dishes. You may use your imagination and experiment with a variety of meals, ranging from proteins and veggies to sweets. To get the most out of their air fryers, encourage your readers to explore and try new things.

✓ First and foremost, safety: Remind your readers to use their air fryers only as directed. They should be instructed to read the instruction booklet in its entirety, handle the basket or trays with oven gloves, and keep kids and pets away from the device while it is in use.

CHAPTER 1

RECIPES FOR BREAKFAST AND BRUNCH

FRENCH TOAST STICKS IN AN AIR FRYER

Serving Size: This dish makes around 4 servings total.

Air Fryer French toast sticks take around 10 to 12 minutes to cook completely.

Preparation Time: This dish requires around 10 minutes of preparation.

Nutrition information:

- ✓ Energy: 230 kcal
- ✓ Fat: 6g

- ✓ 37g of carbohydrates
- ✓ 8g protein
- ✓ 2g of fiber
- ✓ 8g sugar

Ingredients:

- ✓ *8 pieces of bread, your choice of white, whole wheat, or both*
- ✓ *Three big eggs*
- ✓ *0.5 cups of milk*
- ✓ *Vanilla extract, 1 teaspoon*
- ✓ *1/8 teaspoon cinnamon powder*
- ✓ *Greasing the air fryer basket using cooking oil or cooking spray*
- ✓ *Your preferred toppings, such as maple syrup or icing sugar, are optional.*

Directions:

✓ *Your air fryer needs five minutes to reach 350°F (175°C).*

✓ *Eggs, milk, vanilla essence, and powdered cinnamon should all be well blended in a small basin.*

✓ *Depending on your desire, cut each piece of bread into 3–4 sticks of equal size.*

✓ *Make sure each breadstick is well coated on both sides before dipping it into the egg mixture. Any extra mixture should trickle out.*

✓ *To avoid sticking, lightly spritz the air fryer basket with cooking spray or oil.*

✓ *Put the coated bread sticks in the air fryer basket in a single layer. The size of your air fryer will determine whether you need to cook them in batches.*

- ✓ *The French toast sticks should be air-fried at 350°F (175°C) for 5–6 minutes before being turned over using tongs or a spatula.*

- ✓ *The French toast sticks should continue to cook for a further 4-6 minutes to become crispy and golden brown.*

- ✓ *The French toast sticks should be taken out of the air fryer and let to cool for a few seconds.*

- ✓ *With your preferred garnishes, such as maple syrup, confectioner's sugar, or fresh fruit, serve the Air Fryer French Toast Sticks.*

BREAKFAST BURRITOS IN THE AIR FRYER

Size of Serving: two burritos

12–15 minutes for cooking

15 minutes for preparation

Food and nutrition facts (per serving):

- ✓ 400 calories
- ✓ 18g total fat
- ✓ 6g of saturated fat
- ✓ Glucose: 240 mg
- ✓ Salt: 760 mg
- ✓ 35g of carbohydrates
- ✓ 4g of fiber
- ✓ 2g sugars
- ✓ 25g of protein

Ingredients:

- ✓ *Four big eggs*
- ✓ *Milk, 2 tablespoons*
- ✓ *To taste, add salt and pepper.*

- ✓ *Four large wheat tortillas*
- ✓ *12 cups of cheddar cheese, shredded*
- ✓ *1/4 cup sliced bell peppers and 1/2 cup crumbled cooked bacon or sausage*
- ✓ *Diced onions, 1/4 cup*
- ✓ *(Optional, for serving) Guacamole, salsa, or sour cream*

Directions:

- ✓ *For five minutes, heat the air fryer to 350°F (175°C).*

- ✓ *Whisk the eggs, milk, salt, and pepper until fully blended in a medium bowl.*

- ✓ *Spoon a quarter of the egg mixture into the center of a tortilla that has been placed on a spotless surface. It should be uniformly distributed, with a boundary all the way around.*

✓ *On top of the egg mixture, scatter 2 tablespoons of cheddar cheese.*

✓ *Add a tablespoon of each of the chopped bell peppers and onions, then add a quarter of the crumbled bacon or sausage.*

✓ *Make sure the filling is completely encased by folding the tortilla's edges in and rolling it up firmly.*

✓ *With the remaining tortillas and filling ingredients, repeat steps 3-6.*

✓ *Burritos should be placed seam-side down in the air fryer basket without contacting one another.*

✓ *The burritos should be cooked in the air fryer at 350°F (175°C) for 12 to 15 minutes, or until they are crispy and golden brown.*

✓ *Before serving, carefully remove the burritos from the air fryer and allow them to cool.*

✓ *If preferred, top the breakfast burritos cooked in an air fryer with salsa, sour cream, or guacamole.*

BANANA PANCAKES IN AN AIR FRYER

Serving Size: This dish makes around 4 servings total.
10 minutes for preparation
10 minutes for cooking

Food and nutrition facts (per serving):

✓ 210 calories
✓ Fat: 6g
✓ 36g of carbohydrates
✓ 5g protein
✓ 3g of fiber

- ✓ 10g sugar
- ✓ Salt: 310 mg

Ingredients:

- ✓ *2 mashed ripe bananas*
- ✓ *Two huge eggs*
- ✓ *1 teaspoon vanilla essence and half a cup of milk, whether dairy or non-dairy*
- ✓ *All-purpose flour, 1 cup*
- ✓ *1 tablespoon of sugar, granulated*
- ✓ *One tablespoon of baking powder*
- ✓ *1/8 teaspoon cinnamon powder*
- ✓ *A dash of salt*
- ✓ *Greasing the air fryer basket using cooking oil or cooking spray*

Directions:

- ✓ *Set your air fryer's temperature to 350°F (180°C).*

✓ *Combine the mashed bananas, eggs, milk, and vanilla extract in a medium mixing basin. Blend everything well.*

✓ *Combine the all-purpose flour, salt, baking soda, granulated sugar, and ground cinnamon in a separate basin. The dry components should be combined.*

✓ *Stirring occasionally, add the dry ingredients in small amounts to the wet components. Avoid over mixing as this might lead to denser pancakes.*

✓ *To avoid sticking, lightly spritz the air fryer basket with cooking spray or oil.*

✓ *1/4 cup of the pancake batter should be poured into the oiled air fryer basket. Make extra pancakes by repeating the procedure, but spacing them far enough apart to ensure consistent cooking.*

✓ *For around 5 minutes, cook the basket in the preheated air fryer.*

✓ *Use tongs or a spatula to delicately flip the pancakes after five minutes. Cook the pancakes for a further 3– 4 minutes, or until golden brown and well cooked.*

✓ *Transfer the fried pancakes to a serving platter.*

✓ *Warm banana pancakes made in an air fryer should be served with your preferred toppings, such as sliced bananas, berries, maple syrup, honey, or a dusting of powdered sugar.*

EGG AND VEGETABLE MUFFINS COOKED IN THE AIR

This recipe yields 6 muffins as a serving size.

Time spent cooking: around 20 minutes.
15 minutes for preparation.

Food and nutrition facts (per serving):

- ✓ 150 calories
- ✓ 6g of carbohydrates
- ✓ 12g of protein
- ✓ Fat: 9g
- ✓ 2g of fiber
- ✓ 2g sugar
- ✓ Salt: 250 mg

Ingredients:

- ✓ *Six giant eggs*
- ✓ *1/4 cup milk, either dairy or vegan*
- ✓ *Grated cheddar cheese, 1/4 cup*
- ✓ *Any color diced bell peppers, 1/4 cup*
- ✓ *Onions, diced, 14 cup*

✓ *Tomato dice, one-fourth cup*

✓ *1/4 cup of chopped kale or spinach*

✓ *Pepper and salt as desired*

✓ *Olive oil or cooking spray may be used to grease the muffin tins.*

Directions:

✓ *Your air fryer needs five minutes to reach 350°F (175°C).*

✓ *Whisk the milk and eggs together well in a mixing basin. Add salt and pepper to taste.*

✓ *To the egg mixture, include the shredded cheddar cheese, diced bell peppers, onions, tomatoes, and chopped spinach or kale. Completely combine everything.*

✓ *Your air fryer's muffin tins should be greased with cooking spray or a little bit of olive oil.*

✓ *Fill each muffin cup with the egg and veggie mixture equally, approximately 3/4 full.*

✓ *Put the muffin tins in the air fryer basket with care. The size of your air fryer will determine whether you need to cook them in batches.*

✓ *For 12 to 15 minutes, or until the muffins are set and faintly browned on top, set the air fryer to 350°F (175°C). Put a toothpick into the center of a muffin to see whether it is fully cooked. They are prepared if it turns out to be clean.*

✓ *Utilizing oven gloves or tongs, remove the cooked muffin cups from the air fryer. Before serving, let them cool for a while.*

✓ *Warm Air Fryer Egg and Vegetable Muffins are best served. They may be eaten by themselves or with a side of salsa, bread, or a fresh salad.*

BLUEBERRY SCONES IN THE AIR FRYER

Served with six scones.
12–15 minutes for cooking
15 minutes for preparation

Food and nutrition facts (per serving):

✓ 250 calories
✓ Fat: 12g
✓ 32g of carbohydrates
✓ 4g. protein

Ingredients:

✓ *2 cups of general-purpose flour*

✓ *1/4 cup of sugar, granulated*

✓ *Baking powder, two tablespoons*

✓ *1/2 teaspoon salt 1/2 cup cold, cubed unsalted butter*

✓ *50 ml of buttermilk*

✓ *Vanilla extract, 1 teaspoon*

✓ *1 cup of blueberries, fresh*

✓ *Milk, one spoonful (for brushing)*

✓ *(Optional) 1 tablespoon of coarse sugar for sprinkling*

Directions:

✓ *Set your air fryer's temperature to 350°F (175°C).*

✓ *Mix the flour, granulated sugar, baking powder, and salt well in a large mixing basin.*

✓ *To the dry ingredients, add the chilled, cubed butter. Cut the butter into the flour mixture with a pastry cutter or your hands until it resembles coarse crumbs.*

- ✓ *Combine the buttermilk and vanilla essence in another basin. Mix the dry ingredients with the wet mixture just until mixed. Avoid over mixing; the dough should still be a little crumbly.*

- ✓ *Don't bruise the fresh blueberries as you gently fold them in.*

- ✓ *Put the dough on a surface that has been gently dusted with flour. Form it into a disc with a diameter of 1 inch.*

- ✓ *Cut the dough into 6 equal wedges using a sharp knife.*

- ✓ *A parchment-lined air fryer basket or tray should have room between the scones when you place them on it.*

- ✓ *The scones' tops should be brushed with milk, and you may optionally sprinkle them with coarse sugar. They will acquire a lovely golden hue and a mild crunch as a result.*

✓ *Put the scones gently into the air fryer that has been warmed.*

✓ *The scones should be baked for 12 to 15 minutes or until golden brown and done. Depending on the type of your air fryer, the precise cooking time may change, so keep a watch on them.*

✓ *After baking, take the scones out of the air fryer and set them aside to cool on a wire rack.*

✓ *The Air Fryer Blueberry Scones may be served hot or cold. Even while they are delicious on their own, you can also have them with butter, clotted cream, or your favorite jam.*

CHAPTER 2

SNACKS AND APPETIZERS

AIR-FRIED CRISPY CHICKEN WINGS

This recipe makes enough for four people to eat it.

Cooking Time: The whole cooking process takes around 30 minutes.

Time Required for Preparation: Ten minutes or such.

Nutritional value:

- ✓ 2g of carbohydrates
- ✓ 22g of protein

Ingredients:

- ✓ *2 pounds (or 900 grams) poultry wings*
- ✓ *1 teaspoon of baking soda*
- ✓ *1 teaspoon each of salt and paprika*
- ✓ **One-half teaspoon of garlic powder**
- ✓ **One-half teaspoon of onion powder**
- ✓ **Black pepper, 1/4 teaspoon**
- ✓ **Frying oil**

Directions:

- ✓ **The air fryer to 400°F (200°C) of temperature.**

- ✓ **Mix baking powder, salt, paprika, garlic powder, onion powder, and black pepper in a large basin. To make a dry rub, thoroughly combine.**

- ✓ **Using a paper towel, pat the chicken wings dry to get rid of any extra moisture. The success of this phase depends on having crispy wings.**

✓ *Then, throw the wings in the dry rub until they are well covered.*

✓ *To avoid sticking, lightly mist the air fryer basket with cooking spray.*

✓ *Make sure the coated wings are not touching one another when you arrange them in the air fryer basket in a single layer. Depending on the size of your air fryer, you may need to cook the wings in batches.*

✓ *Cook the wings for 20 to 25 minutes in the preheated air fryer, turning them over halfway through. The wings need to be crispy and golden brown.*

✓ *After being cooked, take the wings out of the air fryer and set them aside to rest before serving.*

✓ *For a full supper, serve the crispy air-fried chicken wings with your preferred dipping sauces or next to a side salad.*

CARROT FRIES

This recipe makes enough for four people to eat it.

Time Required for Preparation: Making zucchini fries takes around 15 minutes.

Cooking Time: Zucchini fries take around 20 minutes to prepare.

<u>*Ingredients:*</u>

✓ *Large corvette, two*
✓ *1 cup of breadcrumbs, ideally panko*
✓ *Grated Parmesan cheese, half a cup*

- ✓ 1 teaspoon of powdered garlic
- ✓ Paprika, half a teaspoon
- ✓ 1/4 teaspoon black pepper and 1/2 teaspoon salt
- ✓ 2 big, beaten eggs
- ✓ Olive oil or cooking spray for satisfying

Nutrition information:

- ✓ 200 calories
- ✓ 7g of total fat
- ✓ 2.5g of saturated fat
- ✓ 95 mg cholesterol
- ✓ 540 milligrams of sodium
- ✓ 26g of carbohydrates
- ✓ 2g of fiber
- ✓ Sucrose: 5g
- ✓ 10g of protein

Directions:

✓ *Bake at 425°F (220°C) and line a baking sheet with foil or parchment paper. Apply a thin layer of cooking spray or olive oil to the prepared baking sheet.*

✓ *After giving the zucchini a good wash, trim the ends. Cut the zucchini into long, thin strips that resemble french fries.*

✓ *Combine the bread crumbs, grated Parmesan cheese, paprika, garlic powder, salt, and pepper in a small bowl. Mix well to spread the ingredients evenly.*

✓ *Beat the eggs well in another shallow basin.*

✓ *Each zucchini strip should be uniformly coated with the bread crumbs mixture before being dipped into the beaten eggs, letting any excess drop off. Place the coated zucchini strip on the baking sheet that has been prepared. Continue doing this until all of the zucchini strips have been covered.*

✓ *Olive oil should be gently sprayed or drizzled over the zucchini strips after they have all been coated and put on the baking pan. This will enable them to bake with a crunchy texture.*

✓ *The zucchini fries should be baked in the preheated oven for about 20 minutes or until crispy and golden brown. To achieve equal browning, flip the fries halfway through the baking procedure.*

✓ *After removing the zucchini fries from the oven, give them some time to cool. With your preferred dipping sauce, such as marinara, ranch dressing, or garlic aioli, serve them warm.*

THE CHEESE STICKS

This recipe yields around 20 mozzarella sticks, which serve about 4-6 people.

Cooking Time: Making mozzarella sticks takes 20 to 25 minutes in total.

Time Required for Preparation: It takes around 15 minutes to prepare mozzarella sticks.

<u>*Nutrition value:*</u>

- ✓ 290 calories
- ✓ 15g total fat
- ✓ 9g of saturated fat
- ✓ 55 mg. cholesterol
- ✓ Salt: 750 mg
- ✓ 20g of carbohydrates
- ✓ 18g of protein

<u>*Ingredients:*</u>

- ✓ **Cut up sticks of mozzarella cheese weighing 10 to 12 ounces (280 to 340g).**

- ✓ *All-purpose flour, 1 cup*
- ✓ *1 teaspoon of seasoning mix*
- ✓ *One-half teaspoon of garlic powder*
- ✓ *2 beaten eggs*
- ✓ *Breadcrumbs, 1 cup*
- ✓ *Oil for frying vegetables (optional) Marinara sauce for serving*

Directions:

- ✓ *Create a breading station first. Combine the flour, garlic powder, and Italian seasoning in a single shallow dish. Pour the beaten eggs into a second shallow dish. Place the breadcrumbs in a third dish.*

- ✓ *Each mozzarella stick should be covered in the flour mixture, with any excess being shaken off. Make sure it is well covered with the beaten eggs before dipping it in. To secure the coating, carefully roll the stick in the breadcrumbs. Continue doing this until every mozzarella stick has been covered.*

✓ *On a baking sheet covered with parchment paper, arrange the coated mozzarella sticks and freeze them for approximately 20 minutes. This process aids in the cheese maintaining its form while being fried.*

✓ *In the meanwhile, warm up the vegetable oil in a big pan or pot over medium heat. Make sure the mozzarella sticks are completely submerged in the oil.*

✓ *Once the oil is heated, gently add a few mozzarella sticks and cook them for two to three minutes, or until they are golden brown and crispy. Avoid overcrowding the pot to avoid the sticks sticking together or cooking unevenly.*

✓ *The fried mozzarella sticks should be taken out of the oil with a slotted spoon or tongs and placed on a dish lined with paper towels to absorb any extra oil. Continue doing this with the remaining sticks.*

✓ *Before serving, let the mozzarella sticks cool just a little. Serve them with your favorite dipping sauce or marinara sauce.*

FRIED SWEET POTATOES

Serving Size: This recipe makes enough sweet potato chips for around 4 people.

Prepare Time: 15 minutes for preparing and slicing.

Cooking Period: Bake for 20 to 25 minutes.

Nutrition values:

✓ 142 calories

- ✓ Sodium: 117mg Total Fat: 6g Saturated Fat: 1g
- ✓ 22g of total carbohydrates
- ✓ 4g of dietary fiber
- ✓ 5g sugars
- ✓ 2g protein
- ✓ 440% RDA for vitamin A
- ✓ 3% RDA for vitamin C
- ✓ 4% RDA for calcium
- ✓ 4% RDA for iron

Ingredients:

- ✓ *Two little sweet potatoes*
- ✓ *Olive oil, two teaspoons*
- ✓ *0.5 teaspoons of salt*
- ✓ *0.5 teaspoon of optional paprika (for flavor)*

Directions:

✓ For best results, line a baking sheet with parchment paper and preheat the oven to 400°F (200°C).

✓ To get rid of any dirt or contaminants, properly wash and clean the sweet potatoes. For extra texture and nutrition, keep the skin on.

✓ Round out the thinly sliced sweet potatoes with a mandoline or a sharp knife. Try to make your slices about 1/8 inch thick.

✓ Slices of sweet potato, olive oil, salt, and paprika (if used) should all be combined in a big bowl. Make sure to thoroughly toss and coat each slice with the dressing.

✓ Place the sweet potato slices on the preheated baking sheet in a single layer. To ensure appropriate crispiness while baking, avoid crowding.

✓ *Bake the baking sheet for 10 to 12 minutes in the preheated oven. To achieve equal cooking, take the baking sheet out of the oven after this point.*

✓ *Bake the baking sheet once again in the oven for an additional 10 to 12 minutes, or until the edges of the sweet potato chips are crispy and golden brown. Watch them closely to avoid scorching them.*

✓ *When ready, take the sweet potato chips out of the oven and let them on the baking sheet to cool for a while. They will become even sharper as a result.*

✓ *For the greatest flavor and texture, place the chips on a serving dish or plate and serve right away.*

JALAPENOS IN BACON-WRAPPED POPPERS

Approximately 20 poppers per serving.

25 to 30 minutes for cooking

15-20 minutes for preparation

<u>*Nutrition values:*</u>

- ✓ 140 calories
- ✓ Fat: 11g
- ✓ 2g of carbohydrates
- ✓ 8g protein

<u>*Ingredients:*</u>

- ✓ *10 substantial jalapenos*
- ✓ *8 ounces of softened cream cheese and 10 bacon strips, each split in half*
- ✓ *1/2 cup of cheddar cheese, shredded*
- ✓ *One-half teaspoon of garlic powder*
- ✓ *One-half teaspoon of onion powder*
- ✓ *Paprika, 1/8 teaspoon*

✓ *Pepper and salt as desired*

Directions:

✓ *Turn on the oven to 400 °F (200 °C). For simple cleaning, line a baking pan with aluminum foil or parchment paper.*

✓ *Remove the seeds and membranes from the jalapeno peppers after cutting them in half lengthwise. You may also take off the ribs and the seeds for a milder flavor.*

✓ *Combine the softened cream cheese, shredded cheddar cheese, paprika, onion powder, garlic powder, and salt and pepper in a mixing bowl. All materials should be completely blended after mixing.*

✓ *Place a liberal amount of the cream cheese mixture into each half of the jalapenos.*

✓ *Each packed jalapeno should have a half piece of bacon securely wrapped around it. If necessary, secure it with a toothpick. Continue by using the remaining poppers.*

✓ *On the prepared baking sheet, distribute the bacon-wrapped jalapeno poppers equally.*

✓ *Bake for 25 to 30 minutes in a preheated oven, or until the bacon is crispy and the jalapenos are soft.*

✓ *Once cooked, take the poppers out of the oven and let them cool. Handle them carefully since the filling could be hot.*

✓ *Serve the delicious jalapeno poppers wrapped in bacon as an appetizer. You may eat them on their own or with your preferred dipping sauce, such as ranch dressing or sour cream.*

FRIED EGGS

4 servings per item.

20 to 25 minutes for cooking

30 minutes for preparation

Nutrition value:

- ✓ 190 calories
- ✓ Fat: 8g
- ✓ 24g of carbohydrates
- ✓ 6g protein
- ✓ 2g of fiber
- ✓ 2g sugar
- ✓ Salt: 380 mg

Ingredients:

- ✓ *8 wrappers for egg rolls*
- ✓ *1 cup of cabbage, chopped*

- ✓ 1 cup of carrots, shredded
- ✓ Bean sprouts, 1 cup
- ✓ Chopped green onions, half a cup
- ✓ 2 minced garlic cloves
- ✓ A serving of soy sauce
- ✓ 1 optional tablespoon of oyster sauce
- ✓ Sesame oil, 1 teaspoon
- ✓ A half-teaspoon of black pepper, ground
- ✓ Frying oil for cooking
- ✓ Soy sauce or sweet-and-sour sauce for dipping (optional)

Directions:

- ✓ Shredded cabbage, carrots, bean sprouts, green onions, soy sauce, oyster sauce (if used), sesame oil, and black pepper should all be combined in a big dish. Make sure the ingredients are properly combined and covered evenly.

✓ *One corner of an egg roll wrapper should be facing you when you place it on a spotless surface. Near the bottom corner of the wrapper, place roughly 2 teaspoons of the veggie filling.*

✓ *The bottom corner should be securely folded over the filling. To form an envelope, fold the left and right corners inward. To seal the egg roll, moisten the top corner of the wrapper with water and then roll it up securely.*

✓ *After all the egg rolls have been constructed, repeat the procedure with the remaining wrappers and filling.*

✓ *350°F/175°C) oil should be heated in a deep pan or deep fryer. Several egg rolls at a time, carefully drop them into the heated oil, and cook for 3–4 minutes, or until they are golden brown and crispy. For even cooking, be sure to rotate them periodically.*

✓ *Once cooked, move the egg rolls to a platter covered with paper towels to absorb any remaining oil.*

✓ *While still hot, serve the egg rolls with soy sauce or sweet-and-sour sauce for dipping.*

BITES OF PARMESAN CAULIFLOWER

4 servings per item.
Preparation Time: 25 minutes
15 minutes for preparation

<u>*Nutrition value:*</u>

✓ 180 calories
✓ Fat: 10g
✓ 14g of carbohydrates
✓ 11g of protein
✓ 5g of fiber

Ingredients:

- ✓ 1 cup of breadcrumbs, ideally whole wheat, and 1 medium head of cauliflower
- ✓ 2 big eggs and half a cup of grated Parmesan cheese
- ✓ 1 teaspoon of powdered garlic
- ✓ Paprika, half a teaspoon
- ✓ 14 teaspoons of salt
- ✓ Black pepper, 1/4 teaspoon
- ✓ Frying oil

Directions:

- ✓ For best results, line a baking sheet with parchment paper and preheat the oven to 425°F (220°C).

- ✓ Remove the stiff stem from the cauliflower head and give it a good rinse before cutting it into bite-sized florets.

✓ *Combine the breadcrumbs, grated Parmesan cheese, paprika, garlic powder, salt, and black pepper in a medium bowl. To ensure the flavors are spread equally, thoroughly mix.*

✓ *Beat the eggs well in another basin.*

✓ *A cauliflower floret should be taken, dipped into the beaten eggs, and any excess should fall out.*

✓ *Make sure the floret is well covered in the breadcrumb mixture by rolling it in it. On the baking sheet that has been prepared, put the covered floret. For each floret, repeat this procedure.*

✓ *To help the cauliflower bits get golden brown, lightly mist them with cooking spray.*

✓ *The bits should be crisp and tender after 20 minutes of baking in the preheated oven.*

✓ *After the cauliflower bits are done, remove the baking sheet from the oven and let it cool.*

✓ *As a delightful starter or snack, serve the Parmesan Cauliflower Bites while they are still warm. For more flavor, serve them with your preferred dipping sauce.*

FILLING FOR MUSHROOMS

Serving Size: This recipe makes enough for around 4 people, who will each have an appetizer of 3–4 stuffed mushrooms.

Cooking Time: Stuffed mushrooms take around 25 to 30 minutes to prepare in total.

Preparation Time: This dish requires around 15 minutes of preparation time.

Ingredients:

- ✓ 15 substantial button mushrooms
- ✓ A half-cup of breadcrumbs
- ✓ Grated Parmesan cheese, 1/4 cup
- ✓ 2 teaspoons freshly chopped parsley
- ✓ 2 minced garlic cloves
- ✓ Olive oil, two teaspoons
- ✓ Pepper and salt as desired

Directions:

- ✓ Set your oven's temperature to 375°F (190°C).

- ✓ Clean the mushrooms first. To make a hollow area in the center of each mushroom cap, gently remove the stems. The stems should be saved for subsequent use.

✓ *Combine the breadcrumbs, grated Parmesan cheese, parsley, garlic, olive oil, salt, and pepper in a mixing bowl. All the components should be well mixed.*

✓ *The earlier-reserved mushroom stems should be chopped finely. Mix them well after adding them to the breadcrumb mixture.*

✓ *Place a little amount of the breadcrumb mixture into each mushroom cap and gently push the filling in place.*

✓ *On a baking sheet or in a baking dish, arrange the filled mushrooms.*

✓ *Bake the baking sheet or dish in the preheated oven for 20 to 25 minutes, or until the filling is golden brown and the mushrooms are soft.*

✓ When finished cooking, take the filled mushrooms out of the oven and allow them cool before serving.

✓ The stuffed mushrooms are delicious as an appetizer or as a side dish with your main entrée.

LITTLE PIZZAS

Serving Size: This recipe yields around 12 tiny pizzas, making it perfect to serve as an appetizer or snack for a small party.

Cooking Time: Depending on your oven and preferred degree of crispness, the total cooking time for tiny pizzas is between 15 and 20 minutes.

Mini pizzas need around 10-15 minutes to prepare, including time for assembling the materials and preparing the toppings.

Nutritional Information:

- ✓ Calories: between 100 and 150
- ✓ 4–8 grams of fat
- ✓ Carbs: 10 to 15 grams
- ✓ 4-6 grams of protein
- ✓ Please be aware that depending on the components you use, these figures may not be exact.

Ingredients:

- ✓ *Bagels or little pizza crusts (12 pieces)*
- ✓ *(12 cups) pizza sauce*
- ✓ *(1 cup) of mozzarella cheese, shredded*
- ✓ *Various toppings, including pepperoni slices, bell pepper dice, olive slices, mushrooms, and onions.*
- ✓ *Italian seasoning or dried oregano (optional)*

Directions:

✓ *Start by preheating your oven to the level specified on the container of the tiny pizza crust, or to 400°F (200°C).*

✓ *While the oven is heating, prepare the toppings you want to put on your pizza. Prepare any additional toppings you desire, such as pepperoni slices or chopped veggies.*

✓ **Create the tiny pizzas by arranging the bagels or small pizza crusts on a baking pan covered with parchment paper. Give each crust about a spoonful of pizza sauce, leaving a thin border all the way around. On top of the sauce, sprinkle a layer of shredded mozzarella cheese.**

✓ *Add the garnishes: Now is the time to be imaginative! Each small pizza may have the toppings of your choice. To accommodate varied tastes, you may combine and contrast the elements.*

✓ *Place the baking sheet with the tiny pizzas into the preheated oven to bake them. About 10 to 12 minutes of baking time should be sufficient to melt the cheese, make it bubbly, and brown the crust.*

✓ *Add more dried oregano or Italian spice as a final touch, if preferred, to give the tiny pizzas an additional flavor boost.*

✓ *Prepare and eat: After removing the tiny pizzas from the oven, give them some time to cool. Watch them go as you serve these delectable delicacies as an appetizer or snack.*

GARLIC RINGS

This dish makes plenty for 4 people as an appetizer or snack.

Cooking Time: Onion rings need 20 to 25 minutes to cook completely.

Time Required for Preparation: It takes around 15 to 20 minutes to prepare onion rings.

<u>Nutrition value:</u>

- ✓ 200 calories
- ✓ 10g total fat
- ✓ 2g of saturated fat
- ✓ 25 mg cholesterol
- ✓ Salt: 300 mg
- ✓ 25g of carbohydrates
- ✓ 2g of fiber
- ✓ 4g. protein

<u>Ingredients:</u>

- ✓ **Two big onions**

- ✓ *All-purpose flour, 1 cup*
- ✓ *1 paprika teaspoon*
- ✓ *1 teaspoon of powdered garlic*
- ✓ *1 salt shaker*
- ✓ *Black pepper, half a teaspoon*
- ✓ *Buttermilk, one cup*
- ✓ *2 cups panko-style breadcrumbs*
- ✓ *Frying using vegetable oil*

Directions:

- ✓ **The onions should be peeled and cut into rings that are about 1/2 inch thick. Divide the rings into separate piles.**

- ✓ **Combine the flour, paprika, garlic powder, salt, and black pepper in a shallow dish. Mix well to spread the spices evenly.**

- ✓ **Buttermilk should be placed in another small dish.**

✓ *The breadcrumbs should be placed in a third shallow dish.*

✓ *Each onion ring should be dipped into the flour mixture and thoroughly coated. Clear away any extra flour.*

✓ *After that, dip the buttermilk-coated onion ring into it, letting any extra liquid fall off.*

✓ *Finally, sprinkle breadcrumbs over the onion ring and gently press them into the surface of the onion.*

✓ *For all the onion rings, repeat this procedure.*

✓ *To around 350°F (175°C), heat vegetable oil in a large pan or saucepan. Drop a breadcrumb into the oil to test it. The oil is ready if it sizzles and floats to the top.*

✓ *With caution, add a couple of coated onion rings to the heated oil, taking care not to crowd the pan. The rings should be fried for two to three minutes on each side, or until they are golden brown.*

✓ *Transfer the fried onion rings to a dish with paper towels to absorb any remaining oil using tongs or a slotted spoon. Till all of the rings are done, repeat the frying procedure.*

✓ *As soon as they are hot and crispy, serve the onion rings. You may serve them with your preferred dipping sauces, such as aioli, ketchup, or barbecue sauce.*

CHAPTER 3

RECIPES FOR A MAIN COURSE

CRISPY CHICKEN TENDERS FROM THE AIR FRYER

This recipe makes enough for four people to eat it.

About 15 minutes for cooking

Time spent on preparation: around 15 minutes

Nutrition information:

- ✓ kilocalories: 200
- ✓ 22g of protein
- ✓ 12g of carbohydrates
- ✓ Fat: 7g
- ✓ 2g of saturated fat

- ✓ 75mg of cholesterol
- ✓ Salt: 450 mg
- ✓ 1g of fiber
- ✓ 0g of sugar

Ingredients:

- ✓ *Chicken breasts weighing 1 pound (450 grams), sliced into strips*
- ✓ *All-purpose flour, 1 cup*
- ✓ *2 big, beaten eggs*
- ✓ *Panko breadcrumbs in a cup*
- ✓ *One-half teaspoon of garlic powder*
- ✓ *Paprika, half a teaspoon*
- ✓ *0.5 teaspoons of salt*
- ✓ *Black pepper, 1/4 teaspoon*
- ✓ *Oil or cooking spray for frying*

Directions:

✓ *Set your air fryer's temperature to 400°F (200°C).*

✓ *Set up your breading station in three different bowls.*

✓ *The flour should be put in the first basin. Whisk the eggs in the second dish until well-mixed. Combine the panko breadcrumbs, paprika, garlic powder, salt, and black pepper in the third bowl.*

✓ *Take a chicken strip and shake off any extra flour before coating it. Using the beaten eggs as a dip, coat the floured chicken, letting any extra drop off. To finish, push the chicken into the breadcrumb mixture and coat it well. Repeat with the other chicken strips, placing the breaded chicken strip on a dish after each one.*

✓ *To keep the air fryer basket from sticking, lightly mist or brush it with oil. In the air fryer basket, arrange the breaded chicken tenders in a single layer, ensuring sure they don't touch.*

✓ *After turning the tenders halfway through, place the basket in the preheated air fryer and cook for approximately 10 minutes.*

✓ *The interior temperature of the chicken tenders must reach 165°F (74°C) and become golden brown.*

✓ *Transfer the cooked chicken tenders to a dish covered with paper towels to soak up any extra oil. Before serving, let them cool just a little.*

✓ *With your preferred dipping sauces, such as barbecue sauce, honey mustard, or ranch dressing, serve your crispy air-fried chicken tenders. When served with a side salad or vegetables, they make an excellent appetizer, snack, or even a main entrée.*

AIR-FRIED SALMON WITH DILL AND LEMON

This dish yields enough food for two people.

About 15 minutes for cooking

10 minutes for preparation

<u>*Nutrition value:*</u>

- ✓ 250 calories
- ✓ 30g of protein
- ✓ Fat: 12g
- ✓ 3g of carbohydrates
- ✓ 1g of fiber

<u>*Ingredients:*</u>

- ✓ *2 salmon fillets, each weighing around 6 ounces*
- ✓ *1 lemon*
- ✓ *Olive oil, 1 tbsp.*

✓ One teaspoon dried dill (or one tablespoon chopped fresh dill)
✓ Pepper and salt as desired

Directions:

✓ For around 5 minutes, preheat the air fryer to 400°F (200°C).

✓ To eliminate any extra moisture, blot the salmon fillets dry with a paper towel while the air fryer is getting ready.

✓ Take care to cover both sides of the salmon fillets with olive oil as you drizzle them on. The salmon will be able to maintain moisture and won't stick as a result.

✓ The salmon fillets should be seasoned with salt, pepper, and dried dill. Just before serving, you may garnish the fillets with fresh dill.

✓ *Slice the lemon into small pieces. Place a few lemon slices on top of each salmon fillet and squeeze some lemon juice over the fish.*

✓ *After the air fryer has heated up, gently insert the skin-side-down, seasoned salmon fillets into the air fryer basket.*

✓ *The salmon should be cooked in the air fryer for 10 to 12 minutes, or until it reaches an internal temperature of 145°F (63°C). The thickness of the fillets may affect the precise cooking time. You may boil the salmon for a little less time if you wish.*

✓ *After it has finished cooking, take the salmon out of the air fryer and set it aside to rest before serving.*

✓ *For a satisfying and wholesome supper, top the salmon with more fresh dill and serve it with a side of steamed vegetables or a simple salad.*

VEGGIE QUESADILLAS IN THE AIR FRYER

Size of Serving: 2 quesadillas
15 minutes for preparation
Preparation Time: 12 minutes
Time: 27 minutes in total.

Nutrition information:

- ✓ 250 calories per serving
- ✓ Fat: 10g
- ✓ 32g of carbohydrates
- ✓ 8g protein
- ✓ 5g of fiber

Ingredients:

- ✓ *Four large wheat tortillas*
- ✓ *1 cup of cheese, grated (cheddar, mozzarella, or a combination),*

- ✓ *1 finely sliced tiny red bell pepper*
- ✓ *1 finely sliced tiny yellow bell pepper*
- ✓ *1 small, finely sliced zucchini*
- ✓ *1 finely sliced tiny red onion*
- ✓ *Olive oil, two teaspoons*
- ✓ *1 teaspoon of cumin, ground*
- ✓ *One tablespoon of chili powder*
- ✓ *Pepper and salt as desired*
- ✓ *Sour cream, salsa, and guacamole are optional garnishes.*

Directions:

- ✓ *Set your air fryer's temperature to 375°F (190°C).*

- ✓ *Sliced red and yellow peppers, zucchini, and red onion should all be combined in a big bowl. Olive oil should be drizzled over the dish before cumin, chili powder, salt, and pepper are added. Toss to evenly coat the veggies.*

✓ *Put the seasoned veggies in a single layer in the air fryer basket. Cook the veggies until they are soft and slightly browned for 6 to 8 minutes, shaking the basket halfway through. The air fryer's basket should be taken out and put away.*

✓ *On a tidy surface, spread out two tortillas evenly. Spread out the cheese shreds equally among the tortillas, covering one side of each with them.*

✓ *The cooked veggies should be placed on top of the cheese in a uniform layer.*

✓ *Quesadillas are made by folding the tortillas in half to enclose the filling.*

✓ *Transfer the quesadillas with caution to the air fryer basket that has been heated. Cook the tortillas for 4-5 minutes, or until they are golden brown and the cheese has melted. For even cooking, flip the quesadillas halfway through.*

✓ *After they've finished cooking, take the quesadillas out of the air fryer and let them cool a little before cutting them into wedges.*

✓ *Serve the Air Fryer Veggie Quesadillas hot with your preferred sour cream, salsa, or guacamole.*

PORK CHOPS AIR-FRIED

Two servings per recipe
10 minutes for preparation
15 minutes for cooking

<u>*Nutrition value:*</u>

✓ 260 calories
✓ 32g of protein
✓ Fat: 13g
✓ 2g of carbohydrates

- ✓ 0g of fiber
- ✓ 0g of sugar
- ✓ 90 mg cholesterol
- ✓ 360 mg of sodium

Ingredients:

- ✓ *2 bone-in or boneless pork chops, each approximately 1 inch thick*
- ✓ *Olive oil, 1 tbsp.*
- ✓ *1 teaspoon of powdered garlic*
- ✓ *1 paprika teaspoon*
- ✓ *0.5 teaspoons of salt*
- ✓ *Black pepper, half a teaspoon*
- ✓ *Additional spices of your choosing are optional, such as thyme or rosemary.*

Directions:

- ✓ *For around 5 minutes, preheat your air fryer to 400°F (200°C).*

- ✓ *To remove extra moisture, wipe the pork chops dry with a paper towel while the air fryer is getting ready.*

- ✓ *Salt, black pepper, paprika, garlic powder, and mix in a small bowl. Mix thoroughly.*

- ✓ *The pork chops should be rubbed with olive oil on both sides.*

- ✓ *On both sides of the pork chops, equally, distribute the spice mixture and firmly press it into the flesh.*

- ✓ *Put the seasoned pork chops in a single layer in the air fryer basket. To prevent crowding, if required, fry them in batches.*
- ✓ *The pork chops should be cooked in the air fryer for 12 to 15 minutes, turning them over halfway through. For*

medium doneness, the interior temperature must reach 145°F (63°C).

✓ *After the pork chops have finished cooking, take them out of the air fryer and let them rest before serving.*

✓ *Along with your preferred sides, such as roasted vegetables or a crisp salad, serve the air-fried pork chops.*

SHRIMP WITH COCONUT AIR-FRIED

Serving Size: This dish yields around 4 servings.
Cooking Time: Coconut Shrimp cooked in the air fryer take around 15 minutes to complete.

Preparation Time: This dish requires around 20 minutes of preparation time.

Nutrition value:

- ✓ 235 calories
- ✓ 12g total fat
- ✓ 8g of saturated fat
- ✓ 155 mg of cholesterol
- ✓ Salt: 298 mg
- ✓ 17g of carbohydrates
- ✓ 1g of fiber
- ✓ 2g sugar
- ✓ 15g of protein

Ingredients:

- ✓ *Large prawns weighing 1 pound (450 grams), skinned, deveined, and with tails on*
- ✓ *1 cup of unsweetened coconut shreds*
- ✓ *Panko breadcrumbs in a cup*
- ✓ *All-purpose flour, half a cup*
- ✓ *Two huge eggs*

- ✓ *1 paprika teaspoon*
- ✓ *0.5 teaspoons of salt*
- ✓ *Black pepper, 1/4 teaspoon*
- ✓ *Oil or cooking spray for frying*

Directions:

- ✓ *For a few minutes, preheat your air fryer to 400°F (200°C).*

- ✓ *Panko breadcrumbs and coconut shreds should be combined in a small basin or plate.*

- ✓ *Combine the all-purpose flour, paprika, salt, and black pepper in another shallow basin or dish.*

- ✓ *Lightly beat the eggs in a separate basin.*
- ✓ *Each prawn should be coated three times: once in the flour mixture, once in the beaten eggs, and once more in the coconut and breadcrumb combination. To make*

sure the coating adheres to the prawns, lightly press. For each prawn, carry out the same procedure.

✓ *Making sure they are not crammed together, put the coated prawns in the air fryer basket that has been heated. They may need to be prepared in batches.*

✓ *To help them brown and get crispy, lightly mist or brush the prawns with cooking spray or a little quantity of oil.*

✓ *For even cooking, turn the prawns over halfway through the cooking time of 6 to 8 minutes in the air fryer. They need to be crispy and golden brown.*

✓ *After being cooked, take the prawns out of the air fryer and allow them cool before serving.*

✓ *The Air Fryer Coconut Shrimp may be served as an appetizer or as a main meal. They go well with your choice of tangy dip or sweet chili sauce.*

BBQ CHICKEN DRUMSTICKS IN AN AIR FRYER

Serving Size: This dish makes around 4 servings total.

Cooking period: 25 to 30 minutes.

Time spent preparing: 10 minutes

Nutrition value:

- ✓ 200 calories
- ✓ Fat: 8g
- ✓ 5g of carbohydrates
- ✓ 25g of protein
- ✓ 0.5g of fiber

Ingredients:

- ✓ **8 drumsticks of chicken**
- ✓ **0.5 cups of your preferred BBQ sauce**
- ✓ **1 teaspoon paprika, 2 tablespoons olive oil**
- ✓ **1 teaspoon of powdered garlic**
- ✓ **1 teaspoon of powdered onion**

✓ 1/4 teaspoon black pepper and 1/2 teaspoon salt

Directions:

✓ For around 5 minutes, preheat your air fryer to 400°F (200°C).

✓ Olive oil, paprika, garlic powder, onion powder, salt, and black pepper should all be combined in a small bowl. To make a marinade, thoroughly combine.

✓ Using paper towels, pat the chicken drumsticks to dry. This aids in drying off any surplus moisture from the chicken, giving the skin a crispier texture.

✓ To make sure they are properly covered, brush the marinade on the chicken drumsticks. To improve the flavor, let them marinate for at least 10 minutes.

✓ *Put the drumsticks in the air fryer basket in a single layer. To ensure optimum ventilation, make sure they are not too packed.*

✓ *The drumsticks should be cooked in the air fryer for 20 to 25 minutes, turning them over halfway. To ensure they are fully cooked, use a meat thermometer to test for an internal temperature of 165°F (75°C).*

✓ *After the chicken drumsticks have finished cooking, liberally spray them with your preferred BBQ sauce, covering them completely.*

✓ *To caramelize the BBQ sauce, return the drumsticks to the air fryer and cook for an additional 3 to 5 minutes.*

✓ *Before serving, take the drumsticks out of the air fryer and give them some time to rest.*

✓ *Serve your favorite side dishes, such as coleslaw, potato salad, or grilled veggies, with the succulently crispy and saucy BBQ chicken drumsticks.*

BELL PEPPERS STUFFED IN THE AIR FRYER

4 servings per item.
Preparation Time: 25 minutes
15 minutes for preparation

Nutrition value:

✓ 200 calories
✓ 7g of total fat
✓ 25g of carbohydrates
✓ 10g of protein
✓ 6g of fiber

Ingredients:

- ✓ 4 peppers, any color, bell
- ✓ Cooked quinoa, 1 cup
- ✓ 1 cup washed and drained black beans
- ✓ Corn kernels, 1 cup
- ✓ Tomato dice, half a cup
- ✓ (Optional) 1/2 cup shredded cheddar cheese
- ✓ 14 cups finely minced fresh cilantro
- ✓ 1/9 cup cumin
- ✓ One tablespoon of chili powder
- ✓ One-half teaspoon of garlic powder
- ✓ Pepper and salt as desired

Directions:

- ✓ Set your air fryer's temperature to 375°F (190°C).

- ✓ The bell peppers' tops should be cut off so that the seeds and membranes may be removed. Place aside.

✓ Cooked quinoa, black beans, corn, chopped tomatoes, cilantro, cumin, chili powder, garlic powder, salt, and pepper should all be combined in a mixing dish. To ensure that all components are dispersed equally, thoroughly mix.

✓ Put the quinoa and bean mixture into the bell peppers. Pack the filler by gently pressing it down.

✓ The air fryer basket should be filled with stuffed bell peppers. You may cook them in batches if required.

✓ The filled bell peppers should be cooked in the air fryer for 15 to 20 minutes, or until the peppers are soft and the mixture is well heated.

✓ During the final few minutes of cooking, if preferred, top each filled pepper with shredded cheddar cheese. Let the cheese melt and get a little bit golden.

- ✓ *Before serving, carefully remove the filled bell peppers from the air fryer and allow them to cool.*

- ✓ *Serve the filled bell peppers from the air fryer as a tasty side dish or as a main course with a green salad.*

SALMON TERIYAKI AIR FRYER

This dish yields enough food for two people.
Time spent on preparation: around 10 minutes.
Cooking Time: 12 minutes or such.

<u>*Nutrition value:*</u>

- ✓ Energy: 315 kcal
- ✓ 34g of protein; 16g of fat
- ✓ 7g of carbohydrates
- ✓ 0.5g of fiber
- ✓ Sucrose: 5g

✓ 739 milligrams of sodium

Ingredients:

✓ *2 salmon fillets, each weighing around 6 ounces*

✓ *Low-sodium soy sauce, 1/4 cup*

✓ *Honey, two tablespoons*

✓ *A teaspoon of rice vinegar*

✓ *One teaspoon of sesame oil*

✓ *2 minced garlic cloves*

✓ *1 teaspoon grated ginger*

✓ *Cornflower, one tablespoon*

✓ *1 teaspoon of water*

✓ *(For garnish) Sesame seeds and finely sliced green onions*

Directions:

✓ *For around 5 minutes, preheat your air fryer to 400°F (200°C).*

✓ *To make the teriyaki sauce, combine the soy sauce, honey, rice vinegar, sesame oil, chopped garlic, and grated ginger in a small bowl.*

✓ *Make a slurry by mixing corn flour and water in a different basin. Place aside.*

✓ *Place the salmon fillets skin-side down in a shallow dish or on a plate after patting them dry with a paper towel.*

✓ *Make sure the salmon fillets are uniformly covered by drizzling the fish with half of the teriyaki sauce. Save the leftover sauce for another time.*

✓ *Make sure the salmon fillets are not touching when you put them in the air fryer basket that has been heated.*

✓ *Around 8 minutes to cook.*

✓ *Open the air fryer after 8 minutes and brush the salmon fillets with the teriyaki sauce you saved. Once again, cook them in the air fryer for 4 more minutes, or until the salmon is cooked to the desired doneness.*

✓ *The leftover teriyaki sauce should be warmed up in a small saucepan over medium heat while the salmon is finishing cooking. The sauce will thicken once you add the cornflour slurry and stir. Get rid of the heat.*

✓ *After the salmon has finished cooking, take it out of the air fryer and give it a few seconds to rest.*

✓ *Serve the Air Fryer Teriyaki Salmon with your preferred side dishes or over a bed of steaming rice. Over the salmon, drizzle the thickened teriyaki sauce. Top with sesame seeds and finely chopped green onions.*

✓ *Enjoy the delicious meal of handmade Air Fryer Teriyaki Salmon, which is brimming with flavors and sure to leave you wanting more.*

TURKEY BURGERS IN THE AIR FRYER

Serving Size: This recipe makes enough turkey burgers to serve four people.

Cooking Time: Making Air Fryer Turkey Burgers takes around 15 minutes in total.

The time required to prepare the turkey burgers is around 10 minutes.

Nutrition information:

✓ 250 calories
✓ 12g total fat

- ✓ 2g of saturated fat
- ✓ 100mg cholesterol
- ✓ 350 mg. sodium
- ✓ 5g of carbohydrates
- ✓ 1g of fiber
- ✓ 30g of protein

Ingredients:

- ✓ *1 pound of turkey, ground*
- ✓ *Breadcrumbs, 1/4 cup*
- ✓ *1/4 cup of onion, cut finely.*
- ✓ *1/4 cup bell peppers, chopped finely*
- ✓ *1 minced garlic clove*
- ✓ *A serving of Worcestershire sauce*
- ✓ *One tablespoon of dried parsley*
- ✓ *0.5 teaspoons of salt*
- ✓ *Black pepper, 1/4 teaspoon*
- ✓ *Four whole-wheat hamburger buns*

✓ *Lettuce, tomato, onion, avocado, cheese, and other optional toppings.*

Directions:

✓ **Combine the ground turkey, breadcrumbs, diced bell pepper, diced onion, minced garlic, Worcestershire sauce, dry parsley, salt, and pepper in a large mixing dish. All components should be well combined.**

✓ **Four equal servings of the turkey mixture should be taken. Each part should be formed into an about 3/4-inch-thick patty.**

✓ **For around 5 minutes, preheat your air fryer to 375°F (190°C).**

✓ **Brush a little oil on the air fryer basket or use cooking spray to lightly coat it. Make sure there is space** *between the turkey patties when you place them in the air fryer basket.*

✓ *The turkey burgers should be cooked in the air fryer for 8 to 10 minutes, turning once while cooking, or until an internal temperature of 165°F (74°C) is reached.*

✓ *You might choose to toast the whole wheat burger buns while the burgers are cooking.*

✓ *Once the turkey burgers are cooked, put them on the toasted buns and top them with your favorite ingredients, such as cheese, lettuce, tomato, onion, or avocado.*

AIR FRYER STIR-FRY WITH VEGETABLES

Serving Size: This dish yields around 4 servings.

Cooking Time: The air fryer vegetable stir-fry takes around 15 minutes to prepare.

Preparation Time: This dish requires around 10 minutes of preparation.

Nutrition information:

- ✓ 150 approximately calories
- ✓ Fat: 7g
- ✓ 18g of carbohydrates
- ✓ 5g protein
- ✓ 6g of fiber

Ingredients:

- ✓ *2 cups of various veggies, diced into bite-sized pieces, including bell peppers, broccoli florets, carrots, snap peas, and mushrooms*
- ✓ *Olive oil, 1 tbsp.*
- ✓ *Low-sodium soy sauce, 1 tbsp.*
- ✓ *1 teaspoon of garlic mince*
- ✓ *1 teaspoon of ginger root, grated*
- ✓ *Sesame oil, half a teaspoon*
- ✓ *Pepper and salt as desired*
- ✓ *Optional garnishes: green onions in slices and sesame seeds*

Directions:

- ✓ *For around 5 minutes, preheat your air fryer to 400°F (200°C).*

- ✓ *Olive oil, soy sauce, chopped garlic, grated ginger, sesame oil, salt, and pepper should all be combined in a big bowl. Blend well by whisking.*

✓ *Then, add the mixed veggies to the dish and stir to coat everything with the marinade.*

✓ *Put the marinated veggies in a single layer in the air fryer basket. To prevent crowding, if necessary, sauté the veggies in batches.*

✓ *For an air fryer, cook veggies for 10 to 12 minutes, stirring or shaking the basket halfway through to achieve equal cooking.*

✓ *Remove the veggies from the air fryer as soon as they are cooked through and slightly browned.*

✓ *If desired, add sesame seeds and thinly sliced green onions as a garnish.*

✓ *Serve the air fryer vegetable stir-fry either alone or with steamed rice or noodles as a side dish.*

CHAPTER 4

VEGETABLES AND SIDE DISHES

ZUCCHINI FRIES IN A CRISP

Serving Size: As an appetizer or snack, this dish makes enough for around four people.

Cooking Time: Crispy zucchini fries take around 20 minutes to prepare.

Preparation Time: This dish requires around 15 minutes of preparation time.

Nutrition information:

✓ 120 calories

- ✓ 6g of total fat
- ✓ 1g of saturated fat
- ✓ 0 mg of cholesterol
- ✓ Salt: 240 mg
- ✓ 15g of carbohydrates
- ✓ 3g of fiber
- ✓ 4g sugars
- ✓ 3g. protein
- ✓ 10% of the daily value for vitamin A
- ✓ 35% of the daily value for vitamin C
- ✓ 4% of the daily value of calcium
- ✓ 6% of the daily value of iron

Ingredients:

- ✓ *Two slender zucchini*
- ✓ *All-purpose flour, half a cup*
- ✓ *2 beaten eggs*
- ✓ *1 cup of breadcrumbs, ideally panko*
- ✓ *Grated Parmesan cheese, 1/4 cup*

- ✓ *1 paprika teaspoon*
- ✓ *One-half teaspoon of garlic powder*
- ✓ *Olive oil or cooking spray for frying 1/2 teaspoon salt*

Directions:

- ✓ **Turn on the oven to 425 °F (220 °C). Use olive oil or cooking spray to grease a baking sheet.**

- ✓ **Slice the zucchinis into French-fry-like lengths of long, thin strips. Ensure that they are around 1/2 inch thick.**

- ✓ **Your coating stations should be set up in three different bowls.**

- ✓ **The flour should be put in the first basin. Beat the eggs in a second bowl. The breadcrumbs, grated Parmesan cheese, paprika, garlic powder, and salt should all be combined in the third bowl.**

✓ *Take a strip of zucchini and shake off any extra flour before coating it. Make sure it is well covered by dipping it into the beaten eggs. To help the breadcrumbs stick, carefully press them into the zucchini strip before rolling them in the mixture. Put the oiled baking sheet with the coated strip on it. Continue doing this until all of the zucchini strips are covered.*

✓ *Sprinkle some cooking spray or olive oil over the zucchini strips once they are all placed on the baking pan.*

✓ *The zucchini fries should bake in the preheated oven for 15 to 20 minutes, or until crisp and golden brown. To achieve equal browning, flip them halfway through the cooking process.*

✓ *Before serving, take the zucchini fries out of the oven and let them cool for a while. It is preferable to eat them right away when they are hot and crispy.*

BRUSSELS SPROUTS WITH GARLIC AND PARMESAN

Serving Size: As a side dish, this recipe feeds 4 people.

Cooking Time: It takes around 25 to 30 minutes to prepare the garlic-parmesan Brussels sprouts.

Preparation Time: This dish requires around 10 minutes of preparation.

<u>Nutrition information:</u>

✓ 120 calories
✓ Fat: 6g

- ✓ 11g of carbohydrates
- ✓ 4g of fiber
- ✓ 7g protein

Ingredients:

- ✓ *Brussels sprouts, 1 pound*
- ✓ *Olive oil, two teaspoons*
- ✓ *3 minced garlic cloves*
- ✓ *Grated Parmesan cheese, 1/4 cup*
- ✓ *Pepper and salt as desired*

Directions:

- ✓ *Turn on the oven to 425 °F (220 °C).*

- ✓ *Trim the Brussels sprouts ends and get rid of any outer leaves that are yellowed or damaged. They should be split lengthwise.*

- ✓ *Brussels sprouts cut in half, minced garlic, olive oil, salt, and pepper should all be combined in a big bowl. Make sure the sprouts are uniformly covered by giving them a good toss.*

- ✓ *Spread the Brussels sprouts out in a single layer as you transfer them to a baking sheet.*

- ✓ *The sprouts should be roasted in the preheated oven for 20 to 25 minutes or until crispy and browned. To achieve consistent browning, stir the sprouts halfway during the cooking period.*

- ✓ *Grate some Parmesan cheese over the Brussels sprouts after taking them out of the oven. Lightly toss the sprouts in the cheese to coat them.*

- ✓ *For the cheese to melt and make a thin, crispy crust, place the baking sheet back in the oven for an additional two to three minutes.*

✓ *Serve the Brussels sprouts with garlic and parmesan right away after being taken out of the oven. Warm and crispy are when they are at their finest.*

WEDGES OF SWEET POTATOES

Serving Size: This dish yields around 4 servings.

Cooking Time: Sweet potato wedges take around 30 to 35 minutes to prepare in total.

Preparation Time: This dish takes around 10 minutes to prepare.

Nutrition value:

✓ Calories: between 150 and 200
✓ Carbs: 35 to 40 grams
✓ 2-3 grams of fat

- ✓ 4-5 grams of fiber
- ✓ 2-4 grams of protein

Ingredients:

- ✓ *2 substantial sweet potatoes*
- ✓ *Olive oil, two teaspoons*
- ✓ *1 paprika teaspoon*
- ✓ *One-half teaspoon of garlic powder*
- ✓ *One-half teaspoon of onion powder*
- ✓ *Add salt to taste, about half a teaspoon.*
- ✓ *Black pepper freshly ground (to taste)*

Directions:

- ✓ *Aluminum foil or parchment paper should be used to line a baking sheet while your oven is preheated to 425°F (220°C).*

✓ *Sweet potatoes should be properly washed while maintaining their peel. With a fresh kitchen towel, pat them dry.*

✓ *Sweet potatoes should be cut into wedges that are 1/2 to 3/4 inch thick when cut lengthwise. To achieve consistent cooking, try to make them as uniform in size as you can.*

✓ *Olive oil, paprika, garlic powder, onion powder, salt, and black pepper should all be combined in a big bowl. To make a tasty spice mix, thoroughly combine.*

✓ *Add the sweet potato wedges to the bowl and gently toss them to evenly distribute the spice mixture over each wedge.*

✓ *Leave a little space between each wedge as you arrange the coated sweet potato wedges on the baking sheet that has been prepared.*

✓ *The wedges should be golden brown, crispy on the exterior, and soft on the inside. Place the baking sheet in the preheated oven and bake for 20 to 25 minutes. To achieve equal browning, flip the wedges halfway through cooking.*

✓ *When the sweet potato wedges are perfectly cooked, take them out of the oven and allow them cool before serving.*

✓ *Serve the sweet potato wedges with your preferred dipping sauce or spice as a tasty snack or side dish. Ketchup, garlic aioli, or a sprinkling of fresh herbs like parsley or cilantro are a few of the more well-liked options.*

TEMPURA ONION RINGS

Serving Size: This dish yields around 4 servings.

Cooking Time: It takes around 20 minutes to create crispy onion rings.

The onion rings take roughly 15 minutes to prepare.

Nutrition value:

- ✓ 200 calories
- ✓ 10g total fat
- ✓ Salt: 250 mg
- ✓ 25g of carbohydrates
- ✓ 3g. protein

Ingredients:

- ✓ *Two big onions*
- ✓ *All-purpose flour, 1 cup*
- ✓ *1 paprika teaspoon*

- ✓ One-half teaspoon of garlic powder
- ✓ 1/4 teaspoon black pepper and 1/2 teaspoon salt
- ✓ Buttermilk, one cup
- ✓ Oil from plants (for frying)

Directions:

- ✓ The onions should be peeled and cut into 1/2-inch thick rings. The rings should be separated and placed aside.

- ✓ Combine the all-purpose flour, paprika, garlic powder, salt, and black pepper in a shallow dish. Mix thoroughly.

- ✓ Buttermilk should be added to a different bowl.

- ✓ 350°F/175°C) of vegetable oil in a deep skillet or saucepan is the desired temperature.

✓ *Take an onion ring and cover it completely on both sides in the buttermilk. The extra buttermilk should trickle off.*

✓ *Put the onion ring in the flour mixture and completely coat it. Shake off any extra flour, then place the coated ring on a platter and leave aside. To prepare the remaining onion rings, repeat these steps.*

✓ *A few breaded onion rings should be carefully added one at a time into the heated oil, being careful not to crowd the pan. They should be fried for two to three minutes, or until golden brown.*

✓ *The onion rings should be taken out of the oil with a slotted spoon or tongs and placed on a dish covered with paper towels to absorb any extra oil. Continually sauté onion rings until they are all done.*

✓ *As an appetizer or side dish, serve the crispy onion rings right away with your preferred dipping sauce.*

GARLIC ROASTED CAULIFLOWER

This recipe makes enough for four people to eat it.

Cooking Time: Roasted garlic cauliflower takes a total of 25 to 30 minutes to prepare.

Preparation Time: This dish requires around 10 minutes of preparation.

<u>*Nutrition information:*</u>

✓ 120 calories
✓ 8g of total fat
✓ 1g of saturated fat
✓ 350 mg. sodium

- ✓ 10g of total carbohydrates
- ✓ 4g of dietary fiber
- ✓ 4g sugars
- ✓ 4g. protein
- ✓ 80% of the daily recommended amount of vitamin C
- ✓ 20% of the daily recommended amount of vitamin K

Ingredients:

- ✓ *1 cauliflower head, separated into florets*
- ✓ *4–5 minced garlic cloves*
- ✓ *Olive oil, two teaspoons*
- ✓ *1 paprika teaspoon*
- ✓ *0.5 teaspoons of salt*
- ✓ *Black pepper, 1/4 teaspoon*
- ✓ *(Optional) Fresh parsley for garnish*

Directions:

- ✓ *Turn on the oven to 425 °F (220 °C).*

✓ *Cauliflower florets, minced garlic, olive oil, paprika, salt, and black pepper should all be combined in a big basin. Make sure the cauliflower is fully covered by giving it a good toss.*

✓ *Spread the seasoned cauliflower out in a single layer on a baking pan.*

✓ *Roast the cauliflower on the baking sheet in the preheated oven for 20 to 25 minutes, or until it becomes golden brown and is soft.*

✓ *To achieve consistent browning, stir the cauliflower a couple of times as it cooks.*

✓ *After the cauliflower has been perfectly roasted, take it out of the oven and allow it to cool.*

✓ *If preferred, garnish with fresh parsley and serve immediately.*

FRIES WITH PARMESAN ASPARAGUS

Serving Size: This dish makes around 4 servings total.

Cooking Time: Parmesan asparagus fries take around 20 minutes to prepare in total.

Preparation Time: This dish requires around 10 minutes of preparation time.

Nutrition information:

- ✓ Energy: 110 kcal
- ✓ Fat: 7g
- ✓ 6g of carbohydrates
- ✓ 3g of fiber
- ✓ 8g protein

Ingredients:

- ✓ 1 bunch of spears of fresh asparagus
- ✓ 1/2 cup finely grated Parmesan cheese 1/2 cup normal or panko breadcrumbs
- ✓ 1 teaspoon of powdered garlic
- ✓ 1/4 teaspoon black pepper and 1/2 teaspoon salt
- ✓ 2 beaten eggs

Directions:

- ✓ For best results, line a baking sheet with parchment paper and preheat the oven to 425°F (220°C).

- ✓ Wash the asparagus well, then bend each spear until it breaks naturally to remove the woody ends. Throw out the rough ends.

- ✓ Breadcrumbs, grated Parmesan cheese, garlic powder, salt, and black pepper should all be combined in a small basin. Mix thoroughly.

✓ *Each asparagus spear should be equally covered after being dipped into the beaten eggs. After that, gently push the asparagus as you roll it in the Parmesan breadcrumb mixture.*

✓ *On the prepared baking sheet, arrange the coated asparagus stalks in a single layer, making sure they are not touching.*

✓ *Bake the asparagus fries in the preheated oven for 12 to 15 minutes, or until they are crisp and golden brown.*

✓ *To ensure uniform browning, remember to rotate them once halfway through cooking.*

✓ *After finishing, take the baking sheet out of the oven, and allow the asparagus fries to cool before serving.*

✓ *Serve the Parmesan Asparagus Fries as a wonderful appetizer or side dish. They taste great on their own or when coupled with your favorite dipping sauce, such as marinara or garlic aioli.*

SPANISH STREET CORN

This recipe makes enough for four people to eat it.
Cooking time in total: 20 minutes
Time spent preparing: 10 minutes.

Nutrition value:

- ✓ 180 calories
- ✓ Fat: 7g
- ✓ 28g of carbohydrates
- ✓ 6g protein
- ✓ 3g of fiber
- ✓ Sucrose: 6g

Ingredients:

- ✓ 4 husked ears of corn
- ✓ Mayonnaise, 1/4 cup
- ✓ 1/fourth cup sour cream
- ✓ 1/2 cup coria (or feta) cheese crumbles
- ✓ 50 ml of chili powder
- ✓ Smoked paprika, 1/8 teaspoon
- ✓ 14 cups finely minced fresh cilantro
- ✓ Wedges sliced from 1 lime
- ✓ Pepper and salt as desired

Directions:

- ✓ Heat your grill to a moderately hot setting.

- ✓ Grill the corn: Place the husked corn directly on the grill grates, stir every few minutes, and cook for approximately 10 minutes, or until the corn kernels are soft and just beginning to brown. Take it off the grill, then place it aside.

- ✓ *To make the sauce, put the mayonnaise, sour cream, chili powder, smoked paprika, salt, and pepper in a small bowl and stir until thoroughly blended.*

- ✓ *Coat the corn: Generously brush or pour the sauce mixture over each roasted ear of corn.*

- ✓ *Toppings: Cover the corn with a thin layer of crumbled cotija or feta cheese. Garnish with chopped cilantro after that.*

- ✓ *To serve, spread fresh lime juice over each ear of the Mexican street corn that has been placed on a serving dish. Serving hot, please.*

CRISPY CHIPS WITH EGGPLANT

Serving Size: This dish makes around 4 servings total.

Cooking Time: It takes 20 to 25 minutes to create crispy eggplant chips.

Preparation Time: This dish requires around 15 minutes of preparation time.

Nutrition value

- ✓ Energy: 120 kcal
- ✓ 6g of total fat
- ✓ Salt: 160 mg
- ✓ 15g of total carbohydrates
- ✓ 5g of dietary fiber
- ✓ 3g. protein

Ingredients:

- ✓ *1 large aborigine*
- ✓ *Olive oil, two teaspoons*
- ✓ *1 teaspoon salt 1 optional teaspoon paprika*

✓ *0.5 teaspoons of optional garlic powder*

Directions:

✓ *A baking sheet should be lined with parchment paper or a silicone baking mat and the oven should be preheated to 400°F (200°C).*

✓ *Remove the stem after giving the aubergine a good wash.*

✓ *Slice the aubergine lengthwise into thin, even slices that are 1/4 inch thick. Peeling the aubergine is optional, but the skin gives the chips a lovely texture.*

✓ *Olive oil, salt, paprika, and garlic powder (if used) should all be combined in a big bowl. Make sure each slice of aubergine is well coated in the oil mixture before tossing it in.*

✓ *Place the coated eggplant slices in a single layer, ensuring sure they do not overlap, on the baking sheet that has been prepared. They may crisp up more uniformly as a result.*

✓ **Bake the baking sheet for about 10 to 12 minutes in the preheated oven. The slices should then be turned over and baked for a further 10 to 12 minutes, or until the chips are crispy and golden.**

✓ *Remove the chips from the oven when they are the right degree of crispness and let them cool on the baking sheet for a while.*

✓ *Serve the crunchy eggplant chips alone as a snack or with your favorite dipping sauce or saucer. They may be used as a side dish or as a nutritious alternative to potato chips.*

BAKED POTATOES WITH HERBS

Serving Size: This dish makes around 4 servings total.

Cooking Time: The whole cooking process takes around 40 minutes.

Time Spent Preparing: The preparation process takes around 10 minutes.

Nutrition information:

- ✓ 180 kilocalories
- ✓ 30g of carbohydrates
- ✓ Fat: 5g
- ✓ 4g. protein
- ✓ 4g of fiber
- ✓ Salt: 420 mg

Ingredients:

✓ *Baby potatoes weighing 1.5 pounds (680 grams), cut in half.*

✓ *Olive oil, two teaspoons*

✓ *2 minced garlic cloves*

✓ *1 teaspoon coarsely chopped fresh rosemary*

✓ *One tablespoon of thyme leaves, fresh*

✓ *1 salt shaker*

✓ *1/2 tsp. of black pepper*

Directions:

✓ **Turn on the oven to 425 °F (220 °C).**

✓ **Baby potatoes cut in half, olive oil, chopped garlic, rosemary, thyme, salt, and black pepper should all be combined in a big mixing basin. Toss the potatoes in the herb-infused oil until they are well covered.**

✓ *Spread the seasoned potatoes out in a single layer on a baking sheet or roasting pan. They can cook evenly and become crispy because of this.*

✓ **Roast the potatoes on the baking sheet or in the roasting pan in the preheated oven for 30-35 minutes, or until they are golden and fork-tender. To achieve equal browning, remember to rotate the potatoes halfway during the cooking period.**

✓ **When the potatoes are perfectly roasted, take them out of the oven and allow them cool before serving. This enables them to acquire an additional sharp coating.**

✓ *Place the herb-roasted potatoes on a serving dish and, if you like, top with more fresh herbs. Serve them hot so you can savor their delicious flavors with your preferred main meal.*

GLAZED IN HONEY CARROTS

Serving Size: This dish makes around 4 servings total.

Cooking Time: Carrots coated in honey need 20 to 25 minutes of cooking time.

Time Required for Preparation: Making honey-glazed carrots takes around 10 minutes.

<u>*Nutrition value:*</u>

- ✓ 120 calories
- ✓ 4g of total fat
- ✓ 21g of carbohydrates
- ✓ 4g of fiber
- ✓ 1 g of protein
- ✓ 380% of the daily value for vitamin A
- ✓ 8% of the daily value for vitamin C
- ✓ 4% of the daily value of calcium

✓ 2% of the daily value of iron

Ingredients:

✓ **Carrots weighed 1 pound (450 grams), sliced diagonally.**
✓ **Butter, two tablespoons**
✓ **Honey, two tablespoons**
✓ **1 tablespoon of lemon juice, fresh**
✓ **Pepper and salt as desired**
✓ **Parsley garnish, chopped (optional)**

Directions:

✓ **Prepare the carrots first. They should be peeled and sliced into 1/4-inch-thick diagonal slices. They will cook more evenly and take on a more pleasing shape as a result.**

✓ **Melt the butter in a large pan over medium heat.**

✓ *After the butter has melted, add the carrot slices and cook them in the pan, turning periodically, for approximately 3 to 4 minutes, or until they start to soften.*

✓ *Add the honey, lemon juice, salt, and pepper to the pan after lowering the heat. To ensure that the honey glaze is properly distributed, stir well.*

✓ *Cook the carrots for a further 12 to 15 minutes, or until they are soft but still have a tiny crunch, with the lid on the pan. To achieve consistent cooking and a beautiful glaze coating on the carrots, stir them periodically.*

✓ *Remove the pan from the heat when the carrots are as soft as you want them. If necessary, taste and adjust the seasoning.*

✓ *Place the honey-glazed carrots on a serving dish and, if you like, top with parsley that has been chopped.*

Their eye-catching hues and shiny finish will provide aesthetic appeal.

✓ *The honey-glazed carrots are best served hot as a side dish to your preferred main entrée.*

CHAPTER 5

SWEETS AND DESSERTS

CINNAMON SUGAR DONUTS THAT ARE AIR-FRIED

Size of Servings: This recipe makes around 12 doughnuts.
15 minutes for preparation
10 minutes for cooking

Nutrition value:

- ✓ 140 calories per doughnut
- ✓ 5g total fat
- ✓ 2g of saturated fat
- ✓ 20 mg cholesterol
- ✓ 200 mg. sodium

- ✓ 25g of carbohydrates
- ✓ 1g of fiber
- ✓ 12g sugars
- ✓ 3g. protein

Ingredients:

- ✓ *All-purpose flour, 1 cup*
- ✓ *1/4 cup of sugar, granulated*
- ✓ *One tablespoon of baking powder*
- ✓ *1/8 teaspoon salt 1/8 teaspoon cinnamon, powdered*
- ✓ *14 cups of milk*
- ✓ *One big egg*
- ✓ *2 tablespoons of melted unsalted butter*
- ✓ *Vanilla extract, 1 teaspoon*

For the garnish:

- ✓ *1/4 cup of sugar, granulated*
- ✓ *1 teaspoon of cinnamon powder*

✓ *2 tablespoons of melted unsalted butter*

Directions:

✓ *Set your air fryer's temperature to 350°F (175°C).*

✓ *The flour, brown sugar, baking soda, salt, and ground cinnamon should all be well blended in a large basin.*

✓ *Whisk the milk, egg, melted butter, and vanilla extract until well combined in another basin.*

✓ *After adding the liquid components, mix the dry ingredients just until they are barely blended. Avoid overmixing since it might produce thick doughnuts.*

✓ *Make sure to lightly oil or use cooking spray to grease the air fryer basket.*

✓ *Pour the doughnut batter into a plastic bag with the corner cut off or a piping bag. To create 3-inch doughnuts, pipe the batter into the preheated air fryer. If your air fryer has room for a doughnut pan, you may also use that.*

✓ *The donuts should be cooked in batches for 6 to 8 minutes or until golden brown and springy to the touch. To achieve consistent browning, flip the donuts halfway through the frying process.*

✓ *Prepare the topping by combining the granulated sugar and ground cinnamon in a shallow basin while the donuts are baking.*

✓ *As soon as the donuts are through cooking, take them out of the air fryer and quickly spray each one with melted butter before coating them in the cinnamon sugar mixture.*

✓ *Once all the doughnuts are fried and coated, repeat the procedure with the remaining ones.*

✓ *Before serving, let the donuts cool somewhat. The best way to eat them is warm and fresh.*

AIR-FRIED COOKIES WITH CHOCOLATE CHIPS

Serving Size: This recipe yields around 12 chocolate chip air-fried cookies.
Cooking period: 12 to 15 minutes.
Time spent preparing: 10 minutes

Nutrition value:

✓ 140 calories are included in one cookie.
✓ Fat: 8g
✓ 16g of carbohydrates
✓ 2g protein

- ✓ 1g of fiber
- ✓ 10g sugar

Ingredients:

- ✓ *All-purpose flour, 1 cup*
- ✓ *A half-teaspoon of baking soda*
- ✓ *1/4 teaspoon salt 1/4 cup melted unsalted butter*
- ✓ *1/4 cup of sugar, granulated*
- ✓ *14 cups brown sugar, packed*
- ✓ *One big egg*
- ✓ *Vanilla extract, 1 teaspoon*
- ✓ *Chocolate chips, 1 cup*

Directions:

- ✓ *Your air fryer needs five minutes to reach 350°F (175°C).*

✓ *Combine the flour, baking soda, and salt in a medium basin. Place aside.*

✓ *Cream the softened butter, brown sugar, and granulated sugar in a separate, large mixing bowl until it is light and creamy.*

✓ *Mix the egg and vanilla extract well before adding them.*

✓ *Till a soft dough develops, gradually combine the dry components with the moist ones.*

✓ *After adding the chocolate chips, make sure they are distributed evenly throughout the dough.*

✓ *To avoid sticking, line the air fryer basket with parchment paper or gently oil it with cooking spray.*

✓ *Drop rounded amounts of dough onto the prepared basket using a tablespoon or cookie scoop, allowing room between each cookie for spreading.*

✓ *Cook for 6 to 8 minutes, or until the edges are golden brown and the centers are somewhat soft, in the prepared air fryer with the basket in it.*

✓ *Utilizing tongs or a spatula, carefully remove the cookies from the air fryer. Before serving, let them cool on a wire rack for a while.*

✓ *With the leftover dough, repeat steps 8 through 10 until all of the cookies are baked.*

APPLE FRITTERS, AIR FRIED

Size of Serving: 4 fritters

15 minutes for preparation

10 minutes for cooking

Nutrition values:

- ✓ 170 calories
- ✓ 6g of total fat
- ✓ 1g of saturated fat
- ✓ 0 mg of cholesterol
- ✓ Salt: 160 mg
- ✓ 28g of total carbohydrates
- ✓ 3g of dietary fiber
- ✓ 14g sugars
- ✓ 2g protein

Ingredients:

- ✓ *2 medium-sized apples, chopped after being peeled and cored.*
- ✓ *All-purpose flour, 1 cup*

- ✓ 2 teaspoons of sugar, granulated
- ✓ One tablespoon of baking powder
- ✓ 1/8 teaspoon cinnamon powder
- ✓ 14 teaspoons of salt
- ✓ (Or any other milk of your choosing) 1/2 cup of unsweetened almond milk
- ✓ Vanilla extract, 1 teaspoon
- ✓ Oil mister or cooking spray
- ✓ Dust with optional powdered sugar.

Directions:

- ✓ Set your air fryer's temperature to 350°F (175°C).

- ✓ All-purpose flour, granulated sugar, baking powder, powdered cinnamon, and salt should be combined in a large mixing dish. To blend, thoroughly stir.

- ✓ When the apples are well coated, add the diced apples to the flour mixture and stir.

✓ *Mix the vanilla extract and unsweetened almond milk in another basin. When a thick batter has formed, pour the wet ingredients over the apples that have been dusted with flour.*

✓ *To keep food from sticking, lightly spritz the air fryer basket with oil or use an oil mister.*

✓ *To ensure equal cooking, put about 1/4 cup of the apple batter into the air fryer basket. Space them apart. Depending on how big your air fryer is, you may have to work in batches.*

✓ *The fritters should be cooked for approximately 10 minutes, or until they are golden brown and crispy, at a temperature of 350°F (175°C) in the air fryer. To achieve consistent browning, flip the fritters halfway through the frying procedure.*

✓ *As soon as they are through cooking, gently take the apple fritters from the air fryer basket and set them on a wire rack to cool.*

✓ *Before serving, you may sprinkle the fritters with a little powdered sugar, if you'd like. For added pleasure, you can also serve them warm with a side of vanilla ice cream or caramel sauce.*

CHURROS AIR-FRIED

Serving Size: This recipe makes around 15 churros in total.
Approximately 15 minutes for cooking.
Preparation time: around 15 minutes.

Nutrition values:

✓ 115 calories

✓ 4g of total fat

✓ 2g of saturated fat

✓ 21 mg cholesterol

✓ Salt: 127 mg

✓ 18g of carbohydrates

✓ 0.5g of fiber

✓ 4g sugar

✓ 2g protein

Ingredients:

✓ *One water cup*

✓ *2 teaspoons of sugar, granulated*

✓ *2 tablespoons vegetable oil and 1/2 teaspoon salt*

✓ *All-purpose flour, 1 cup*

✓ *2 big eggs and 1 teaspoon of vanilla extract*

✓ *Frying oil*

✓ *(For coating) 2 tablespoons of granulated sugar*

✓ *1 teaspoon cinnamon powder (for coating).*

Directions:

- ✓ *Mix the water, sugar, salt, and vegetable oil in a medium pot. Over medium heat, bring the mixture to a boil while stirring periodically.*

- ✓ *Add the flour after taking the pan off the heat. Use a wooden spoon to stir the ingredients briskly until it comes together into a smooth dough that pulls away from the pan's edges.*

- ✓ *Once the dough has cooled for approximately five minutes, transfer it to a mixing bowl.*

- ✓ *For around 5 minutes, preheat your air fryer to 375°F (190°C).*

- ✓ *Mix the vanilla essence well into the dough after adding it.*

✓ *One egg at a time, beat the dough well after each addition until it's glossy and smooth.*

✓ *The dough should be transferred into a piping bag with a big star tip.*

✓ *To avoid sticking, lightly spray cooking spray on the air fryer basket.*

✓ *Churros should be piped into the air fryer basket with room between them to ensure equal cooking. Churros should be around 4-5 inches long.*

✓ *At 375°F (190°C), air-fried the churros for 8–10 minutes, or until crispy and golden brown. To achieve equal browning, turn the churros over halfway through the frying process.*

✓ *Transfer the churros to a platter covered with paper towels while they are still warm to drain any extra oil.*

- ✓ For the coating, mix the ground cinnamon and granulated sugar in a small basin.

- ✓ To uniformly coat the heated churros, roll them in the cinnamon-sugar mixture.

- ✓ Serve the air-fried churros right away with your preferred dipping sauce, such as caramel or chocolate ganache.

AIR-FRIED HAND PIES WITH BLUEBERRIES

Serving Size: This dish yields around 4 servings.
Cooking time in total: 20 minutes
15 minutes for preparation

Nutrition values:

- ✓ 180 calories

- ✓ Fat: 7g
- ✓ 27g of carbohydrates
- ✓ 3g. protein
- ✓ 2g of fiber

Ingredients:

- ✓ *1 cup of blueberries, fresh*
- ✓ *2 teaspoons of sugar, granulated*
- ✓ *1/8 cup lemon juice*
- ✓ *Two frozen pre-made sheets of puff pastry, one beaten egg (for egg wash),*
- ✓ *Sugar in powder form (for dusting)*

Directions:

- ✓ *Set your air fryer's temperature to 375°F (190°C).*

- ✓ *The blueberries, granulated sugar, and lemon juice should all be combined in a small bowl. Some of the* blueberries may be gently mashed to release their juices and improve the mixture. Place aside.

✓ Unfold the puff pastry sheets on a surface dusted with a little flour. Cut out circles with a glass or a round cookie cutter that are about 4-5 inches in diameter.

✓ Fill the center of each circle with a tablespoon of the blueberry filling, leaving a thin border all the way around.

✓ Don't overfill it since it can spill out when cooking.

✓ The pastry rounds should be folded in half to create a semicircle. To crimp the pies' edges and seal them tight, use a fork.

✓ To give the pies' tops a golden color when cooked, brush them with beaten egg wash.

✓ *Make sure there is space between the hand pies when you put them in the air fryer basket. Whenever required, cook in batches.*

✓ *The pies should be air-fried at 375°F (190°C) for 10 to 12 minutes, or until crisp and golden brown.*

✓ *After cooking, take the hand pies out of the air fryer and let them cool for a moment.*

✓ *To give the pies a delicious finishing touch, sprinkle them with powdered sugar.*

AIR-FRIED SPRING ROLLS WITH BANANAS

This recipe makes enough for four people to eat it.

Cooking Time: Air-fried banana spring rolls take 15 to 20 minutes to prepare.

Preparation Time: This dish requires around 10 minutes of preparation.

Nutrition values:

- ✓ 180 kilocalories
- ✓ 38g of carbohydrates
- ✓ Fat: 3g
- ✓ 2g protein
- ✓ 2g of fiber
- ✓ Sucrose: 18g

Ingredients:

- ✓ *Four ripe bananas*
- ✓ *8 wrappers for spring rolls*
- ✓ *Brown sugar, 2 tablespoons*
- ✓ *1 teaspoon of cinnamon powder*
- ✓ *Oil or cooking spray for air frying*
- ✓ *For serving, you may use powdered sugar or honey.*

Directions:

✓ Set your air fryer's temperature to 400°F (200°C).

✓ Bananas should be peeled and split in half lengthwise. Put them apart.

✓ Combine the brown sugar and ground cinnamon in a small bowl.

✓ On a spotless surface, spread out a spring roll wrapper. A substantial quantity of the cinnamon-sugar mixture should be sprinkled on top of the diagonally positioned banana half.

✓ The wrapper should be folded over the banana on the sides before being securely rolled like a burrito. To seal the wrapping, dab a little water over the edges.

✓ With the remaining spring roll wrappers and bananas, repeat the procedure.

✓ To avoid sticking, lightly mist or brush cooking oil or spray over the air fryer basket.

✓ Make sure the prepared banana spring rolls are in the air fryer basket in a single layer and are not touching.

✓ The spring rolls should be air-fried at 400°F (200°C) for 10 to 12 minutes, turning them halfway through, or until golden brown and crispy.

✓ When finished, take the spring rolls out of the air fryer and set them aside to cool.

✓ Warm Air Fried Banana Spring Rolls may be drizzled with honey or dusted with powdered sugar if desired.

AIR-FRIED M&Ms

Air Fried Smokes are served in portions of four using this recipe.

Time required for cooking: around 5 minutes

Time spent on preparation: around 10 minutes

Nutrition values:

✓ 220 calories

✓ 9g total fat

✓ 4.5g of saturated fat

✓ 5 mg of cholesterol

✓ Salt: 130 mg

✓ 33g of carbohydrates

✓ 1g of fiber

✓ 17g sugars

✓ 3g. protein

Ingredients:

- ✓ *Breaking eight Graham crackers in half*
- ✓ *4 substantial marshmallows*
- ✓ *2 chocolate bars, cut up into tiny pieces (such as Hershey's).*

Directions:

- ✓ *For a few minutes, preheat your air fryer to 375°F (190°C).*

- ✓ *A slice of chocolate should be placed on top of a graham cracker half. Put a marshmallow on the chocolate after that.*

- ✓ *To make a sandwich, take another graham cracker half and put it on top of the marshmallow.*

- ✓ *To create a total of 4 s'mores sandwiches, repeat this procedure with the remaining graham crackers, marshmallows, and chocolate.*

✓ *To avoid any sticking, line the air fryer basket with parchment paper or use a baking dish made for air fryers.*

✓ *S'mores should not touch when they are being placed in the air fryer basket or baking dish.*

✓ *The marshmallows should be golden brown and gooey after cooking for around 4-5 minutes in the air fryer that has been warmed. Carefully insert the basket or dish into the air fryer.*

✓ *Due to differences in air fryer models and marshmallow sizes, it is important to keep a careful check on the s'mores while they cook.*

✓ *When finished, use tongs or a spatula to remove the hot s'mores from the air fryer.*

✓ *Before serving, let the s'mores cool for a few seconds.*

- ✓ *Enjoy the ooey-gooey goodness of these wonderful Air*

- ✓ *Fried S'mores by serving them while they're still warm!*

LEMON POPPY SEED MUFFINS FRIED IN THE AIR

Servings per Recipe: This recipe yields around 12 muffins.
20 minutes for cooking
15 minutes for preparation

Nutrition values:

- ✓ 180 calories
- ✓ Fat: 7g
- ✓ 27g of carbohydrates
- ✓ 4g. protein

Ingredients:

- ✓ All-purpose flour, 1 1/2 cups
- ✓ Granulated sugar, half a cup
- ✓ 1 tablespoon poppy seeds and 1 tablespoon lemon zest
- ✓ Baking powder, two tablespoons
- ✓ 1/2 tsp. baking soda
- ✓ 4 grains of salt
- ✓ Buttermilk, 1/4 cup
- ✓ 14 cups melted unsalted butter
- ✓ One big egg
- ✓ 1 tablespoon of lemon juice, fresh
- ✓ Vanilla extract, 1 teaspoon

Directions:

- ✓ For a few minutes, preheat your air fryer to 350°F (175°C).

- ✓ The flour, sugar, poppy seeds, lemon zest, baking soda, and salt should all be well mixed in a large mixing basin.

✓ *Whisk the buttermilk, melted butter, egg, lemon juice, and vanilla extract in a separate basin.*

✓ *After adding the liquid components, mix the dry ingredients just until they are barely blended. Avoid over mixing; a few lumps are OK.*

✓ *Use muffin liners to coat the air fryer basket or gently grease it with non-stick spray. Distribute the batter equally among the muffin liners, filling each one to approximately two-thirds full.*

✓ *In the air fryer that has been warmed, put the muffin-filled basket. When a toothpick is pushed into the center of a muffin, it should come out clean after about 12 to 15 minutes of cooking.*

✓ *When the muffins have finished cooking, take them from the air fryer and allow them cool in the basket for a while. After that, move them to a wire rack to finish cooling.*

FRIED RASPBERRIES IN THE AIR

This recipe yields around 6 turnovers per serving.
Cooking time in total: 20 minutes
15 minutes for preparation

Nutrition values:

- ✓ 196 calories
- ✓ Fat: 10g
- ✓ 25g of carbohydrates
- ✓ 2g protein
- ✓ 2g of fiber

Ingredients:

- ✓ One box (17.3 ounces) of thawed frozen puff pastry
- ✓ 1 cup raspberries, either fresh or frozen
- ✓ 1/4 cup of sugar, granulated
- ✓ Corn flour, one tablespoon
- ✓ One-half teaspoon of vanilla extract
- ✓ 1 beaten egg for the egg wash
- ✓ Dusting with powdered sugar is optional.

Directions:

- ✓ Set your air fryer's temperature to 375°F (190°C).

- ✓ The raspberries, granulated sugar, corn flour, and vanilla essence should all be combined in a medium bowl.

- ✓ Gently swirl the sugar mixture until the raspberries are completely covered. For the raspberries to release their juices, let the filling rest for a while.

✓ *Roll out the thawed puff pastry to a thickness of about 1/8 inch on a surface that has been gently dusted with flour. Depending on the size of the turnover you want, cut the pastry into squares or rectangles.*

✓ *Place one to two teaspoons of the raspberry filling in the middle of each piece of pastry. Making a triangle, fold the crust diagonally over the filling. Using a fork, seal the turnover by pinching the edges together.*

✓ *Apply the beaten egg wash to the turnovers' tops. They'll acquire a lovely golden hue as a result.*

✓ *Place the turnovers in the air fryer basket, allowing room between each one to allow for airflow. The size of your air fryer will determine whether you need to cook them in batches.*

✓ *The turnovers should be air-fried for 8 to 10 minutes, or until puffed and golden brown. For even browning, flip them halfway through cooking.*

✓ *When the turnovers are finished cooking, gently take them from the air fryer and let them cool on a wire rack for a while.*

✓ *Dust the turnovers with powdered sugar, if desired, to provide an added sweetness.*

✓ *Warm up the air-fried raspberry turnovers before serving and savor the mouthwatering contrast between the flaky pastry and rich raspberry filling.*

AIR-FRIED LITTLE PIES OF APPLES

Servings: four little apple pies.

20 minutes for preparation

12–15 minutes for cooking

Nutrition values:

- ✓ 160 calories
- ✓ Fat: 7g
- ✓ 23g of carbohydrates
- ✓ 3g of fiber
- ✓ 2g protein

Ingredients:

- ✓ *2 medium-sized apples, either Honey crisp or Granny Smith*
- ✓ *2 teaspoons of sugar, granulated*
- ✓ *1 teaspoon of cinnamon powder*
- ✓ *1/4 teaspoon of nutmeg, ground*
- ✓ *One teaspoon of lemon juice*
- ✓ *1/9 cup all-purpose flour*

- ✓ *2 sheets of frozen pre-made puff pastry, 1 beaten egg,*
- ✓ *Dusting with powdered sugar is optional.*

Directions:

- ✓ *Set your air fryer's temperature to 375°F (190°C).*

- ✓ *The apples should be diced, peeled, and cored. Diced apples, sugar, cinnamon, nutmeg, lemon juice, and flour should all be combined in a bowl. Mix well until the apples are equally covered.*

- ✓ *Puff pastry sheets should be rolled out to a thickness of approximately 1/8 inch on a lightly dusted surface. Cut out circles with a glass or a round cookie cutter that are about 4 inches in diameter.*

- ✓ *Each pastry circle should have a tablespoon of apple filling in the center. To create a half-moon shape, fold the circular in half and seal the edges by pressing them together.*

✓ *For a decorative touch, crimp the edges using a fork.*
✓ *The small pies' tops should be brushed with the beaten egg to give them a glossy, golden sheen.*

✓ *Make sure the small apple pies are not touching one another when you arrange them in the air fryer basket in a single layer. You may have to cook them in batches depending on the size of your air fryer.*

✓ *The pies should be air-fried for 12 to 15 minutes, or until crisp and golden brown. Watch them carefully to avoid over-browning.*

✓ *After they have finished cooking, gently take the tiny apple pies from the air fryer and allow them to cool. If desired, sprinkle with powdered sugar.*

✓ *Serve the air-fried little apple pies hot or cold. They are delectable on their own, but for an extra special treat, try serving them with a scoop of vanilla ice cream or a dollop of whipped cream.*

CHAPTER 6

DIPS AND SAUCES

CONVENTIONAL MARINARA SAUCE

Serving Size: Depending on the meal you're making, this recipe makes enough marinara sauce to serve around 8 people or about 4 cups.

Cooking Time: Making traditional marinara sauce takes around one hour in total.

The traditional marinara sauce takes around 15 minutes to prepare.

Nutrition values:

- ✓ Calories: Each serving (1/2 cup) has around 80 calories.
- ✓ Fat: 3g
- ✓ 11g of carbohydrates
- ✓ 2g protein
- ✓ 3g of fiber
- ✓ 400 mg. sodium

Ingredients:

- ✓ *Olive oil, two teaspoons*
- ✓ *1 small onion, diced finely*
- ✓ *4 minced garlic cloves*
- ✓ *One 28-ounce can of chopped-up tomatoes*
- ✓ *One 14-ounce can of tomato ketchup*
- ✓ *6 ounces in one can of tomato juice*
- ✓ *One tablespoon of dried basil*
- ✓ *Oregano, dry, 1 teaspoon*
- ✓ *0.5 teaspoons of sugar*
- ✓ *Pepper and salt as desired*
- ✓ *Fresh basil leaves may be used as a garnish.*

Directions:

✓ *In a large saucepan set over medium heat, warm the olive oil. Add the chopped onion and cook for approximately five minutes, or until it becomes translucent and slightly golden. Occasionally stir to avoid scorching.*

✓ *When aromatic, add the minced garlic to the pan and simmer for an additional one to two minutes.*

✓ *Add the tomato paste, tomato sauce, and crushed tomatoes. To thoroughly incorporate all the ingredients, stir well.*

✓ *Add sugar, salt, pepper, dried oregano, and dried basil. To fully mix the ingredients into the sauce, stir once more.*

✓ For around 45 minutes, reduce the heat to low, cover the pan, and stir the sauce regularly.

✓ This will enable the sauce to thicken and the flavors to mingle.

✓ Liking the sauce after it has simmered for a while, and then season to your liking. If necessary, increase the amount of salt, pepper, or herbs.

✓ Use an immersion blender or transfer the sauce to a conventional blender to purée the sauce until it is smooth if you desire a smoother consistency. This step is not necessary since traditional marinara sauce often has a little chunky texture.

✓ Remove the sauce from the heat once it gets the consistency you like. Fresh basil leaves may be used as a garnish to provide freshness and flavor.

✓ *Your beloved Italian recipes may now be prepared with your traditional marinara sauce. Any leftovers may be kept in the refrigerator for up to a week in an airtight container.*

THE HOT BUFFALO DIP

Serving Size: This dish yields around 8 servings.

Cooking Time: Making Spicy Buffalo Dip takes around 25 minutes in total.

Preparation Time: Making a Spicy Buffalo Dip takes around 10 minutes.

Nutrition values:

✓ 200 calories
✓ 16g total fat

- ✓ 8g of saturated fat
- ✓ 45 mg. cholesterol
- ✓ Salt: 800 mg
- ✓ 5g of carbohydrates
- ✓ 8g protein

Ingredients:

- ✓ *8 ounces of softened cream cheese*
- ✓ *A half-cup of ranch dressing*
- ✓ *50% of a cup of buffalo sauce*
- ✓ *1 cup of cooked chicken, shredded, and 1 cup of cheddar cheese, shredded*
- ✓ *14 cups finely chopped green onions*
- ✓ *Serving of tortilla chips, celery, or carrot sticks*

Directions:

- ✓ *Turn on the oven to 350 °F (175 °C).*

✓ *Buffalo hot sauce, ranch dressing, and softened cream cheese should all be combined in a mixing basin. Stir well to get a smooth mixture.*

✓ *To the bowl, add half of the shredded cheddar cheese and the cooked chicken that has been shredded. Mix everything until it's all spread equally.*

✓ *Spread out the mixture equally in a baking dish that has been buttered.*

✓ *Over the dip, top with the remaining cheddar cheese, shredded.*

✓ *For around 15-20 minutes, or until the cheese is melted and bubbling, bake the dip in the preheated oven.*

✓ *The dip should be taken out of the oven and given some time to cool.*

✓ If desired, add finely chopped green onions as a garnish for visual appeal.

✓ With tortilla chips, celery sticks, or carrot sticks for dipping, serve the spicy buffalo dip warm.

SOUR BBQ SAUCE

This recipe makes around 2 cups of tangy BBQ sauce, which is the serving size.

Cooking Time: This dish requires 25 to 30 minutes of total cooking time.

Preparation Time: Making this zesty BBQ sauce takes around 10 minutes.

Nutrition values:

✓ Each serving (2 tablespoons) has 50 calories.

✓ 0 g of total fat

✓ Salt: 170 mg

✓ 13g of carbohydrates

✓ 11g sugars

✓ 1 g of protein

Ingredients:

✓ *Ketchup, 1 cup*

✓ *A quarter cup of apple cider vinegar*

✓ *Quarter cup brown sugar*

✓ *Worcestershire sauce, two teaspoons*

✓ *1/9 cup Dijon mustard*

✓ *1 teaspoon of honey*

✓ *A serving of soy sauce*

✓ *Smoked paprika, 1 teaspoon*

✓ *One-half teaspoon of garlic powder*

✓ *One-half teaspoon of onion powder*

✓ *Black pepper, half a teaspoon*

✓ *Cayenne pepper, 1/4 teaspoon (adjust to taste)*

Directions:

✓ *Combine the ketchup, apple cider vinegar, brown sugar, honey, soy sauce, Worcestershire sauce, Dijon mustard, garlic powder, onion powder, black pepper, and cayenne pepper in a medium pot.*

✓ *Make sure the brown sugar is thoroughly dissolved when you whisk the ingredients together.*

✓ *Bring the mixture to a moderate boil in the saucepan over medium heat. Stirring periodically, lower the heat to low and simmer for 15 to 20 minutes.*

✓ *The flavors will mix delightfully as the sauce simmers and gently thickens.*

✓ *After simmering, turn off the stove and let the spicy BBQ sauce cool to room temperature.*

✓ *Transfer the sauce to a jar or other airtight container after it has cooled. It lasts for up to two weeks in the refrigerator.*

✓ *You may now use your tangy BBQ sauce to marinate, baste, or serve as a dipping sauce for your preferred grilled meats, hamburgers, chicken wings, or veggies.*

GARLICKY AIOLI IN CREAM

This recipe yields around 1 cup (16 tablespoons) of creamy garlic aioli, which is the serving size.

10-minute total cooking time

5 minutes for preparation

Nutrition values:

- ✓ 120 calories
- ✓ 13g total fat
- ✓ 2g of saturated fat
- ✓ 15 milligrams of cholesterol.
- ✓ Salt: 130 mg
- ✓ 1 g of carbohydrates overall
- ✓ 1 g of protein

Ingredients:

- ✓ *Mayonnaise, one cup*
- ✓ *3-4 minced garlic cloves*
- ✓ *One teaspoon of lemon juice*
- ✓ *Dijon mustard, 1 teaspoon*
- ✓ *Salt, as desired*
- ✓ *Pepper, as desired*

Directions:

✓ *Mayonnaise, minced garlic, lemon juice, and Dijon mustard should all be combined in a small basin. All of the components should be properly combined after mixing.*

✓ *To taste, add salt and pepper to the food. Start with a little quantity and increase it as needed to reach your preferred level.*

✓ *Keep in mind that you can always add additional seasoning afterward, but it might be difficult to get rid of too much salt or pepper.*

✓ *The aioli mixture should be stirred until it turns creamy and smooth. Mayonnaise will absorb the flavors of the garlic, producing a wonderfully fragrant sauce.*

✓ *Once the aioli is well combined, taste it and, if required, adjust the spice. For a stronger garlic flavor, add more* minced garlic; for a tangier flavor, add more lemon juice.

✓ Before serving, transfer the aioli to an airtight container and chill for at least 30 minutes. During this cooling period, the flavors might converge and the aioli can somewhat thicken.

✓ Your favorite foods should be served with the Creamy Garlic Aioli. It tastes great with fries, chicken tenders, roasted veggies, sandwiches, burgers, and even as a dip for crudité platters.

SWEET & SOUR

This recipe makes roughly 1 cup of honey mustard, which is the serving size.

10 minutes for preparation

Cooking Time: Not necessary

Nutrition values:

- ✓ 70 calories
- ✓ 4g of total fat
- ✓ 0.5g of saturated fat
- ✓ 5 mg of cholesterol
- ✓ 120 milligrams of sodium
- ✓ 8g of total carbohydrates
- ✓ 0g of dietary fiber
- ✓ 7g sugars
- ✓ 1 g of protein

Ingredients:

- ✓ *50 ml of mayonnaise*
- ✓ *One-fourth cup of Dijon mustard*
- ✓ *Honey, 1/4 cup*
- ✓ *One teaspoon of lemon juice*

✓ *A quarter-teaspoon of garlic powder*
✓ *Pepper and salt as desired*

Directions:

✓ *Mayonnaise, Dijon mustard, honey, lemon juice, garlic powder, salt, and pepper should all be combined in a mixing bowl.*

✓ *The honey mustard sauce will be smooth after all the ingredients have been well combined.*

✓ *After tasting the mixture, add more salt, pepper, or honey as desired.*

✓ *You may add a little water and whisk again to get the correct consistency if you'd like it to be thinner.*

✓ *Transfer the honey mustard sauce to a fresh container or jar that has a tight-fitting lid.*

✓ Before serving, put the sauce in the refrigerator for at least 30 minutes to enable the flavors to blend.

✓ Serve the homemade honey mustard as a dressing for salads and sandwiches, or use it as a dip for vegetables, pretzels, or chicken tenders. It is also excellent as a marinade or with grilled meats.

YUMMY TZATZIKI

Serving Size: This recipe makes about 2 cups of tzatziki, with 1-2 tbsp. per serving.

Cooking Time: Not necessary.

Tzatziki preparation takes between 10 and 15 minutes.

Nutrition values:

- ✓ 35 calories
- ✓ 2g of total fat
- ✓ 1g of saturated fat
- ✓ 3 mg of cholesterol
- ✓ 42 milligrams of sodium
- ✓ 3g of carbohydrates
- ✓ 0g of fiber
- ✓ 2g sugar
- ✓ 2g protein

Ingredients:

- ✓ *1 big cucumber, grated after being peeled*
- ✓ *Greek yogurt in two cups*
- ✓ *2 minced garlic cloves*
- ✓ *Extra virgin olive oil, 1 tablespoon*
- ✓ *1 tablespoon of lemon juice, fresh*
- ✓ *1 teaspoon dried dill or 1 tablespoon minced fresh dill*
- ✓ *1 tablespoon finely minced fresh mint leaves*
- ✓ *Pepper and salt as desired*

Directions:

✓ Using a box grater or food processor, grate the cucumber first. After being granted, transfer the mixture to a fine-mesh strainer or a clean dish towel, and squeeze off the surplus liquid. By doing this, you can keep your tzatziki from becoming watery.

✓ Greek yogurt, minced garlic, extra virgin olive oil, lemon juice, dill, and mint leaves (if used) should all be combined in a medium bowl. To ensure the flavors are spread equally, thoroughly mix.

✓ Once the grated cucumber has been added, whisk the yogurt mixture well. The shredded cucumber gives the tzatziki a cool crunch.

✓ To your taste, add salt and pepper, and adjust the seasoning to suit your preferences. Remember that *because yogurt already has some natural saltiness, add a little salt at first and then more if necessary.*

✓ *Once everything is well combined, cover the bowl and chill the tzatziki for at least one to two hours in the refrigerator to let the flavors blend.*

✓ *Give the tzatziki a brief toss before serving and taste to see if the seasoning needs to be changed. For extra aesthetic appeal, you may top it with a drizzle of olive oil and some fresh herbs.*

✓ *With pita bread, fresh veggies, grilled meats, or as a dipping sauce for sandwiches and wraps, tzatziki is best-savored cold.*

CHIPOTLE CREAM DIP

This recipe makes around 1.5 cups of creamy chipotle dip, which is the serving size.

Cooking Time: The Creamy Chipotle Dip takes around 10 minutes to prepare in total.

Preparation Time: This dip takes around 5 minutes to prepare.

Nutrition values:

- ✓ 90 calories are included in each serving.
- ✓ Fat: 8g
- ✓ 4g of carbohydrates
- ✓ 1 g of protein
- ✓ 1g of fiber

Ingredients:

- ✓ *Mayonnaise, one cup*

- ✓ 1/fourth cup sour cream
- ✓ 1-2 minced chipotle chiles in adobo sauce from a can
- ✓ 1 tablespoon of adobo sauce (made from chipotle chiles in a can)
- ✓ 1 minced garlic clove
- ✓ A teaspoon of lime juice
- ✓ 1/8 teaspoon cumin powder
- ✓ Pepper and salt as desired

Directions:

- ✓ Mayonnaise, sour cream, minced chipotle peppers, adobo sauce, minced garlic, lime juice, ground cumin, salt, and pepper should all be combined in a mixing dish. Make sure all the ingredients are well mixed together.

- ✓ Once you've tasted the dip, season it to your liking. Add extra minced chipotle peppers or adobo sauce to make

*it hotter. Reduce the number of chipotle peppers for a
milder flavor.*

✓ *Transfer the dip to a serving dish as soon as you're
happy with the flavor.*

✓ *If you have time, chill the dip in the fridge for at least
30 minutes before serving. This will enable the flavors
to combine and improve the overall flavor.*

✓ *Serve the Creamy Chipotle Dip with your preferred
snacks, including tortilla chips, pretzels, veggie sticks,
or even as a topping for sandwiches or burgers.*

TERIYAKI GLAZE, TANGY

Serving size: around one cup
15 minutes for cooking
5 minutes for preparation

Nutrition values:

- ✓ 60 calories
- ✓ 0 g of total fat
- ✓ 0 mg of cholesterol
- ✓ Salt: 680 mg
- ✓ 14g of total carbohydrates
- ✓ 11g sugars
- ✓ 1 g of protein

Ingredients:

- ✓ *50 ml of soy sauce*
- ✓ *A mug of water and a mug of brown sugar*
- ✓ *Rice vinegar, two teaspoons*
- ✓ *Honey, two tablespoons*
- ✓ *1 tablespoon of garlic, minced*
- ✓ *1 tablespoon ginger root, chopped*
- ✓ *1 tablespoon of optional thickening corn flour*
- ✓ *A tablespoon of optionally added sesame oil*

Directions:

- ✓ *Soy sauce, water, brown sugar, rice vinegar, honey, ginger, and garlic powder should all be combined in a small pot. To blend, thoroughly stir.*

- ✓ *Stirring periodically, bring the mixture to a simmer in the saucepan over medium heat. To enable the flavors to mingle, let it simmer for around 5 minutes.*

- ✓ *In another bowl, whisk together the corn flour and one tablespoon of water to make a thicker glaze if you wish.*

- ✓ *Stir constantly, and gradually add the cornflour mixture to the pan. Cook for a further 2 minutes, or until the glaze reaches the desired thickness.*

- ✓ *After turning off the heat, remove the pot and let the glaze some time to cool.*

✓ *If desired, whisk in sesame oil to the glaze. Although it gives an additional flavor dimension, sesame oil is optional.*

✓ **The Tangy Teriyaki Glaze is prepared for use after it has cooled. You may use it as a marinade for tofu or chicken, or you can drizzle it over grilled meats and stir-fried veggies. It is excellent as a brush-on sauce for skewered meats as well as a dipping sauce.**

SMOOTH RANCH DIP

Servings: This recipe makes about 2 cups of creamy ranch dip, which serves 8 to 10 people.

Preparation Time: This dip takes around 10 minutes to prepare.

Cooking Time: There is no need to prepare the creamy ranch dip. The major step of the procedure is combining the materials.

<u>**Nutrition values:**</u>

- ✓ 70 calories
- ✓ 7g of total fat
- ✓ 2g of saturated fat
- ✓ 10 mg cholesterol
- ✓ 180 milligrams of sodium
- ✓ 2g of carbohydrates
- ✓ 1 g of protein

<u>**Ingredients:**</u>

- ✓ *1 cup soured milk*
- ✓ *50 ml of mayonnaise*
- ✓ *50 ml of buttermilk*
- ✓ *1 tablespoon coarsely chopped fresh chives*

- ✓ 1 tablespoon coarsely chopped fresh dill
- ✓ 1 teaspoon freshly chopped fresh parsley
- ✓ 1 teaspoon of powdered garlic
- ✓ 1 teaspoon of powdered onion
- ✓ 1/4 teaspoon black pepper and 1/2 teaspoon salt

Directions:

- ✓ Combine the sour cream, mayonnaise, and buttermilk in a medium mixing basin. Stir vigorously until completely smooth and combined.

- ✓ Chives, dill, and parsley should be chopped and added to the mixture. To evenly distribute the herbs throughout the dip, thoroughly mix.

- ✓ Add the salt, black pepper, onion powder, garlic powder, and so on. To ensure that all the ingredients are dispersed equally, gently stir.

✓ *After mixing, either place plastic wrap over the bowl or transfer the dip to an airtight container. To give the flavors a chance to mingle, chill for at least one hour.*

✓ *Give the dip one more swirl just before serving to bring any separated ingredients back together. Garnish with more fresh herbs, if preferred.*

✓ *Along with your preferred chips, crackers, veggies, or other munchies, serve the creamy ranch dip. Additionally, it works well as a delicious topping for baked potatoes as a salad dressing.*

CHILLI SAUCE SWEET

✓ *This recipe makes around 1 1/2 cups of sweet chili sauce, which is the serving size.*

✓ *Cooking period: 25 to 30 minutes.*

✓ *15 to 20 minutes for preparation*

Nutrition values:

✓ Size of serving: 1 tbsp.

✓ 45 calories

✓ 0 g of total fat

✓ Salt: 210 mg

✓ 11g of carbohydrates

✓ 10g sugar

✓ 0g protein

Ingredients:

✓ *1 cup sugar, granulated*

✓ *Rice vinegar, one cup*

✓ *14 cups of water*

✓ *2 teaspoons minced garlic*

✓ *2 teaspoons of red pepper flakes, tasted,*

✓ *10 ml of fish sauce*

- ✓ Corn flour, one tablespoon
- ✓ One tablespoon of chilled water

Directions:

- ✓ *The sugar, rice vinegar, water, chopped garlic, red chili flakes, and fish sauce should all be combined in a pot. To ensure that the sugar dissolves fully, stir well.*

- ✓ *Bring the mixture to a moderate boil in the saucepan over medium heat. Allow the mixture to simmer for 10 to 15 minutes on low heat to let the flavors blend.*

- ✓ *Corn flour and cold water should be combined to make a slurry in a small bowl. Pour the slurry into the pan while continually stirring. The sauce will thicken as a result.*

- ✓ *Until the sauce reaches the appropriate consistency, simmer it for a further 5-7 minutes on low heat, stirring often. Glossy and slightly thickened, the sauce should be.*

✓ *The sweet chili sauce should cool to room temperature once the pot has been taken from the heat.*

✓ *When the sauce has cooled, put it in a glass jar or other airtight container and store it in the refrigerator. As it cools, the sauce will become thicker yet.*

✓ *You may now enjoy your sweet chili sauce! Use it as a glaze for grilled meats and veggies or as a dipping sauce for spring rolls and chicken nuggets.*

Printed in Great Britain
by Amazon

28966026R00112